S0-AFX-950

Secrets

OF THE

PROPHETIC

Unveiling Your Future

Secrets

OF THE
PROPHETIC

Unveiling Your Future

KIM CLEMENT

Previously published as *The Sound of His Voice* (ISBN 088419339X),
© 1993 Charisma House

© Copyright 2005 – Kim Clement
All rights reserved. This book is protected by the copyright laws
of the United States of America. This book may not be copied or
reprinted for commercial gain or profit. The use of short quota-
tions or occasional page copying for personal or group study is permitted and encouraged. Permission will be granted upon request.
Unless otherwise identified, Scripture quotations are from the New
King James Version, copyright © 1982 by Thomas Nelson, Inc. Used
by permission. All rights reserved. Scriptures marked TLB, KJV,
NASB, NIV, and NRSV are taken from the The Living Bible, King
James Version, New American Standard Bible, New International
Version and New Revised Standard Version, respectively. Please
note that Destiny Image's publishing style capitalizes certain pro-
nouns in Scripture that refer to the Father, Son, and Holy Spirit,
and may differ from some Bible publishers' styles.
Take note that the name satan and related names are not cap-
italized. We choose not to acknowledge him, even to the point of
violating grammatical rules.

Destiny Image® Publishers, Inc.
P.O. Box 310
Shippensburg, PA 17257-0310

"We Publish the Prophets"

ISBN 0-7684-2312-0

For Worldwide Distribution
Printed in the U.S.A.

This book and all other Destiny Image, Revival Press, MercyPlace,
Fresh Bread, Destiny Image Fiction, and Treasure House books
are available at Christian bookstores and distributors worldwide.

5 6 7 8 9 10 11 12 13 14 / 11 10 09 08 07 06

For a U.S. bookstore nearest you, call **1-800-722-6774**.
For more information on foreign distributors, call **717-532-3040**.
Or reach us on the Internet:
www.destinyimage.com

ENDORSEMENTS

"Kim Clement brings to this work a history, a perspective, and a passion that is usually lacking in most books on the prophetic. I believe this work is destined to become a classic and should be read by anyone who is searching for ancient answers to contemporary questions. This is a timely book for troubled times."

Dr. Myles E. Munroe
BFM International
Nassau, Bahamas

"Kim Clement has been a great blessing to the TBN family, and to Jan and me personally, for many years. So I was honored when he asked me to endorse his new book, *Secrets of the Prophetic*. In this book you will meet the man behind the message, and you will discover that Kim's life synchronizes with his ministry. If you are longing to gain insights into the prophetic word, then this book will lead you on the pathway to that discovery. I recommend, without hesitation, both the man and his ministry."

Paul F. Crouch
President
Trinity Broadcasting Network

"Kim Clement has truly impacted both my life and business as a dear friend and minister of the gospel. His ministry has been a great source of prophetic insight to our family for many years. I am honored to endorse his new book, *Secrets of the Prophetic*. This book sheds light into both the life and message of a true prophetic voice. I believe that when the principles found in this book are applied, it can help you find great success in your family, your business, and your ministry."

Peter Lowe
CEO and Creator of Get Motivated Seminars

CONTENTS

ACKNOWLEDGMENTS

JESUS—without Jesus, we are empty canisters. Thank You for being there before I was born and believing in me.

Gloria, my faithful mother-in-law and servant of God—you are certainly the glutenous factor that keeps everything together, aside from the bread that you bake.

Jane, my wife—who has lived with a prophet and a man. Most people see the prophet; she sees and knows the man as well. You are a virtuous woman, and this is the strength of the prophetic voice.

My children—each one of you was born at a specific moment in my life, adding momentum and reason for the future. You are the future; you are tomorrow's voice that I live and fight for.

My team—thank you for your strength and for your life. Finally someone was able to put it all together for me. When you say you're working after hours—you are. You are a reward to me.

To my dear friend Dan Gatti—thank you for loving me and watching over my life and business. You are indeed a friend of God.

FOREWORD
BY ORAL ROBERTS

Why I Believe This Book Will Help You

Kim Clement, a young man from South Africa, was searching for God, for His way out of defeat and confusion, and could find no one who believed he could ever be a true man of God. Consequently, he sat down and wrote to me in Tulsa, asking, "Can you help me?" What he really meant was, "*Will* you help me?"

We studied his few handwritten words, looked over our books and tapes and sent them to him as a *seed* sown into his life, not knowing we would ever actually meet him. It was just another seed of our faith that came from God's revelation to me on "The Miracle of Seed-Faith." The rest was up to Kim. Soon others were helping him who had refused before, possibly because they began to see a change in him.

It's inspiring to read Kim's story and to witness what a tremendous man of God he is now, and is still becoming.

If you need help in finding a change of direction or for new doors to open to you or to better learn how to not look to people who won't or can't help you, then start looking to your only true SOURCE. I believe you will bless the day you read Kim's book, *Secrets of the Prophetic*.

Oral Roberts
Chancellor
Oral Roberts University

PREFACE

One of the major concerns I have is the fact that most people are completely aware of the fact that the "Word"—Jesus Christ—is living inside of them. They boast about it, shout about it, sing about it, and yet they act like heathen when persecution or adversity arises. They call out for prophets, leaders, and other spiritual gurus to "lead" them and show them a way out. The dreaded plague of "escapism" is consuming any chance of greatness for a future generation and teaching our children that departure from a problem is the answer. It is not!

A departure mandate has replaced the biblical and historical Dominion mandate—which starts in Genesis and fills the pages with heroes who fought and took occupation and ends at a rugged cross with the Hero of Golgotha snatching the kingdom of darkness from under satan's nose. Yes, He was tempted, as we all are, to escape the unavoidable confrontation with the religious and demonized masses, the self-sacrifice and pain, but He took His honorable place and uttered "nevertheless, Your will be done."

Jesus' prayer "Your Kingdom come" is often ignored and replaced with "Your King come *now* (and take us away from this horrible earth)." We forget that "the earth is the Lord's and the fullness thereof" (Ps. 24:1 KJV), or what about "Your will be done *on earth* as it is *in heaven?*" (Matt. 6:10). God's divine will has always been to *occupy* territory. He told the children of Israel that they had to dispossess their enemies before they could possess the land (see Num. 33:53).

Today when we find an adversary on our promised land, we ask for a way of escape. What a shame! Every believer who has been born again has the right to *see* and *enter* the Kingdom of God while on earth! The prophetic word that lives inside of you can only be manifest once it has become a voice. You are the voice! Shakespeare wrote, "My voice is in my sword." In other words, actions speak loudly—louder than words sometimes.

A truly prophetic person is led by the Spirit, filled with the Spirit, and empowered by the Spirit. My best explanation of this is in Matthew 4:1, where Jesus is "*led by the Spirit*" to be tempted by the devil! The word inside of you must become a voice (a manifestation). After Jesus had taken occupation of His territory by overcoming temptation, He became a voice—in the temple, at the feast, in Jerusalem to the Jews and the Gentiles, at the tomb of Lazarus, and yes, even on the cross. Satan could *not shut him up.* Even when Jesus never uttered a word—He was a voice.

This book will teach you the ways of God and how to recognize His voice and will challenge you to become a voice on the earth—a voice that has the distinct sound of *God* in it.

CHAPTER ONE

A SHATTERED DREAM

I'm only seventeen, and I'm dying, I thought, as I pressed my hand against my chest, trying in vain to stop the blood that was flowing from a deep stab wound near my shoulder.

I staggered to the bathroom of that rock club in Port Elizabeth, South Africa, and everything around me became a giant blur. My mind was so drugged with alcohol and dope that I didn't even know who had stabbed me—or why.

"Isn't anyone going to help me?" I cried, as I stuffed paper towels inside my shirt to fight the hemorrhaging. But no one heard me. I was alone.

I lurched out of the bathroom, struggled through the crowded club, and fell on my face in the gutter outside. *Everybody here knows me,* I thought, *but nobody cares.*

As a musician I had headlined in that club countless times. My name had been plastered in the papers because of a movie contract I had just signed with an Australian film company. Even that very night the people were congratulating me.

No one knew it, but my life had actually reached a point of hopelessness and despair. Everything I tried seemed so exciting at the start, but with each success, emptiness arose in the pit of my stomach, something that I could not explain. Twice that same month I had tried to take my own life. Now it seemed as if someone had done it for me.

Is this how it is going to end? I thought. *Is my life over?*

CRACKING MY KNUCKLES

In 1956, I was born in Uitenhage, South Africa. Uitenhage was a town of about 50,000 people on the outskirts of the city of Port Elizabeth. It is a coastal area about halfway between Cape Town and Durban.

My father, Vivian, had a government job with the housing department of the railways, and my mother, Babette, worked at odd jobs to help make a living for the family. I was the second of four children—three boys and a girl. We lived in a modest, but comfortable, brick home at 10 Butler Street, which was on a hill that overlooked the Uitenhage railroad station.

Like most white South African families, we had a black maid who came to work every day from the segregated township where she lived. Her name was Hilda, and even though she was African, she was like a second mother to me.

As far back as I can remember, my parents told me, "Kim, you are going to be a classical pianist." In fact, they insisted that all of us—my two brothers, my sister, and I—be trained in music.

When I was five I started piano lessons with my Aunt Belle. It was a painful experience. She was a demanding teacher and would strike my knuckles with a pencil if I made a mistake. But before long I played "After the Ball" at a recital. Then my mother enrolled me in classical music at the local branch of Trinity College of London. It was a rigorous program that included an annual musical examination.

Every day I would practice two or three hours on our old upright piano, and by the time I was nine or ten, my motivation was no longer external. I *wanted* to practice. I craved to perform. And I began to believe that I was destined to be an outstanding musician. I dreamed about performing great concerts and traveling the world.

Once my mother took me to a fortune-teller who told me, "Young man, I see that you will one day go overseas as a musician and become famous."

Going to a clairvoyant was nothing unusual in our home. We were a Christian family only in the broadest sense of the term. I certainly did not have a God-fearing upbringing. The only time we visited the local Methodist church was to meet some friends or to attend a wedding or a funeral.

Yes, we believed there was a God. Yes, we celebrated Christmas. But we were never encouraged to read the Bible or to know the side of Christianity that emphasized a relationship with Jesus Christ. We barely even knew the religious side.

To say that we were a liberal family is an understatement. By the time I was 9 I was smoking, and my parents never stopped me. It's not that my mother and father were evil or immoral people—they just wanted their children to be "free" and expressive.

I can still remember what happened after I had an unfortunate accident in our home when I was about 10 years old. While my parents were asleep, early one morning my brother and I were fooling around on the roof and I fell. When I hit the ground, I stopped breathing and was rushed to the hospital. The damage to one of my hips was so severe that I was under medical care for nearly three months.

One day an Anglican minister, wearing his clerical collar, came into my hospital room. He walked over to my bed and asked, "Would you like me to pray with you?"

"No," I instinctively responded, "I don't want any prayer." Then he looked me straight in the eye and said something that never left me, "Jesus still walks the streets today, and one day you are going to need Him. If you call on Him, He'll walk over to you, and He will touch you."

I didn't respond to his words, and he quietly left the room.

FORBIDDEN FRIENDS

When I was 11, I told my mother, "I'm through with classical music. You can forget about any more lessons." I had discovered other styles of music—and I was drawn in.

Jazz was just a brief fling before rock music became the new force that dominated every waking moment of my life. I listened to it on the radio, bought cassette tapes, and began to play it on my Korg keyboard. My new desire was to become a rock star.

I used to go to Port Elizabeth to hear almost every rock group that came into town. I didn't have to sneak out of the house. That wasn't necessary. My parents let me do my own thing.

That same year I began playing in my first rock band. We were called "Mark IV."

Growing up in South Africa in the 1960s and 1970s, I was surrounded by conflict and strife. In every direction there was hate and mistrust.

Many of our neighbors were shocked that some of my best friends were blacks—all of them musicians. The controversy grew when I performed with a "colored" rock group named "The Invaders." I thought nothing about venturing into black townships where whites were forbidden because my friends lived there.

Most of the world sees the problem of South Africa as a political struggle between blacks and whites. But the roots of the hostility run much deeper. In reality, the clash includes black against black and white against white.

In my own home, for example, great hatred existed toward Afrikaners—white people of Dutch descent. We learned to speak Afrikaans, the "kitchen Dutch" language that was spoken in our community. But we detested it. At home we spoke only English.

Whites make up only about 18 percent of the population, but they are divided into two distinct camps. Three-fifths are

Afrikaners, and the remainder are English. Their strife stems from the war fought at the turn of the century between the Boers, or Dutch farmers, and the Uitlanders, or "foreigners" (who were mainly British). Each had settled huge geographical areas of the territory. The stakes were high. The world's largest gold and diamond mines had been discovered, and a bitter struggle for power ensued. Even though the forces of Great Britain prevailed, and the Union of South Africa was established in 1910, the hatred and mistrust continues to this day.

A conflict also exists between the blacks and the "coloreds," the part-white descendants of several African peoples who mingled with the first white settlers. They are the most rejected people in the country and are despised by tribal blacks.

Asians, mainly from India, make up only 3 percent of the population, but they also live in a constant state of turmoil. The Africans hate the Asians and the Hindus hate the Muslims. And the Indian Christians are the target of even more antagonism.

South Africa is the only major nation in the world where a racial minority controls the government. In 1948, *apartheid* became the official law of the land. It is an Afrikaans word meaning "apartness." Its aim was to keep the four main racial groups (whites, blacks, coloreds, and Asians) strictly separated— socially and politically.

Apartheid laws affected every aspect of life in South Africa. Although 73 percent of the population is black, they were severely restricted regarding where they could live, where they could work, and the education they could receive. Even the church became an extension of apartheid. From pulpits across the land white ministers preached that the Bible endorses separation of the races.

The historic riots in the native housing areas of Soweto and Sharpsville were, in large part, ignited by the attempt to force the black population to learn the Afrikaans language.

In America, racial segregation was symbolized by signs on the seats of public buses that read, "Blacks only beyond this point." In South Africa, the entire bus was segregated. Signs on drinking fountains and rest rooms said, "Whites only"—and often no facilities existed at all for blacks.

The response from the world community was one of moral outrage. Economic sanctions and sports boycotts attempted to isolate the country politically. But inside the country, even after social apartheid laws were officially abolished, the cauldron continued to boil. People wondered if democracy would prevail and if the rule of the white minority would end with a bloodbath.

It was not to be. On February 2, 1990, then-President F.W. de Klerk gave a famous speech to Parliament that led to Nelson Mandela's release and the fall of apartheid. In April 1994, the first-ever democratic elections took place, and Nelson Mandela became president, thus bringing an end to centuries of racial segregation and abuse.

AN INCORRIGIBLE TRUANT

At the age of 13, I didn't care about such weighty matters as African nationalism or racial politics. I was a young rebel, and I couldn't care less what others thought. I regularly used marijuana and bragged about it. Every few months my friends and I would form a new music group. One of them, the Purple Fez, was punk rock, so we all dressed in outlandish purple outfits.

At the heart of everything we did was a rebellion against authority. I was always the youngest member of the group, running with a fast crowd in their late teens and early twenties.

Our great idols were Led Zeppelin, Jimi Hendrix, Janis Joplin, and Deep Purple. We would not only listen to their tapes, but we'd try to dress like them and copy their stage movements—even take the same drugs.

My older brother Barry played the trumpet, and he joined our rock group at the places where we played. We began to get bookings everywhere—from golf clubs and pubs to colleges. Soon we were playing venues in Port Elizabeth, East London, and Cape Town. Then came "The Cosmic Blues." It was the show band—an 18-piece rock group that played to audiences that numbered in the thousands. I was on the keyboard/synthesizer and did some of the vocals.

What about my education? I was expelled from three different schools because I was so unruly. Somehow I felt like a misfit who didn't belong. I was in a society where the blacks were rejected, yet they were my friends. The English white people were rejected, yet they were my family.

It wasn't only school that I hated. Except for my music, I hated everything about the first 17 years of my life. Educational authorities labeled me as an incorrigible truant because I would stay away from school for weeks at a time.

Above our house were two hills. At the top of one of them was a public park with a sizable monument in honor of King George V, the monarch who was on the throne when the Union of South Africa was formed. Standing at the base of the monument provided a great view of the entire town of Uitenhage.

Once, for a period of about three weeks, I climbed that hill every morning and just sat there, desperately unhappy. I would wait for my parents to leave for work, then go back to the house, take my drugs, and listen to my collection of rock music. The school authorities finally picked me up, and the principal gave me "six of the best"—with a cane.

The problem became even more serious when the officials found drugs on me. I was expelled. My parents could not find any school in our town that would admit me. They finally took me to Port Elizabeth and enrolled me in the Lawson Brown School. The headmaster, after hearing my story and calling the principal in Uitenhage, said, "Look, I know you have a problem, but we are going to take a chance on you." Then he added, "As a Christian, I feel that is the least I can do."

It was obvious that my rebellious streak was like a wild horse that would not be tamed. The drug use and pattern of truancy continued until I was eventually asked to leave. Before my 17th birthday I was a druggie who had turned to the "hard stuff." I became addicted to heroin, and my life seemed to be vanishing before me.

South Africa is very strict about drug use, but I knew where to obtain drugs and still stay out of trouble with the authorities. No cocaine was available at that time, but I had a source for heroin. And with the money I was making in music, I was able to afford it.

In the Finals

I remember the day my mother came to me and said, "Kim, there is something I think you should do."

"Go ahead. Tell me what it is," I responded.

She showed me the promotional brochure for an international music competition being held in Port Elizabeth. "I believe you can win the best keyboard artist category, and then you would represent South Africa in the finals in Japan." Yamaha sponsored the event.

It was obvious why my mother wanted me to enter the contest. It was her chance to show her friends that all my early music training had not been wasted and that I was a serious musician after all. So I told her, "If it will make you happy, I'll do it."

The contest turned out to be a major event. I succeeded in the preliminary rounds and was in the spotlight in the finals that were held at the city hall. The format of the competition was unique, to say the least. Each contestant performed for about eight minutes until he or she was stopped by a loud bell.

That night, however, I was so drugged and drunk when I was playing that I never did hear that bell. I just kept going until one of the judges walked over and stopped me. Of course, the judges realized that I was on some kind of drug—and my dress code left much to be desired. They awarded me second place. Two newspaper critics and a magazine columnist who wrote that I should have won it all, however, consoled my bruised ego.

I lost. But in the audience was a film producer from Australia who had flown in to shoot some footage along the South African coast. His crew was filming a movie called *A Winter's Tale.* To my surprise, the producer approached me with a proposal. "We'd really like you to do some original music for this movie," he said.

"Great! Cool man!" I was pumped up about this opportunity.

Immediately I began to immerse myself in the project. I felt as if it was going to be my big break. The newspapers wrote about how this young man from Uitenhage was hired to score the music for a motion picture. It was an important event for our family.

Financially, the contract was generous. I was scheduled to travel to Australia for the film's premier. "You don't know how lucky you are," my friends told me.

But once again I felt absolutely empty and miserable. I would practice for several hours and then turn to drugs. I felt as if my life was spinning out of control. It was a cycle I could not seem to break—despite two major events that should have shaken me to my core.

SELF-INFLICTED INJURIES

One evening I came to my house and had a seizure—obviously from a bad combination of drugs. All I remember was grabbing a knife with a long blade from the kitchen. Then I blanked out. When I gained my sense, I realized I was cutting myself repeatedly in my stomach. Blood was everywhere. It was as if I was trying to kill myself without my consciousness knowing it.

A few weeks later that same feeling came over me. I didn't know anything about satan at the time, but I sensed that an evil power was attempting to possess my life. Perhaps the devil knew that something unusual was about to happen, and he wanted to torment me—even kill me.

Another time I was listening to a recording of *Jesus Christ Superstar*. I played it again and again even though it made me miserable. The more I heard it, the more agitated I became. *Who is this Jesus?* I asked myself. *And why are these people singing about Him?*

While the record was playing, I again felt that my actions were being controlled by a great, diabolical power. I blacked out. And when I came around, I was horrified to realize that I had taken the mouthpiece from my brother's trumpet and was stabbing at my eye and my forehead with the small part of it. The blood was flowing down my cheek and onto my shirt. There were small cuts and wounds all over my head. Something was going terribly wrong.

It was obvious that I was desperate to have something dramatically change the course of my life.

"Is It Over?"

One evening I stopped working on the film project and decided to hang out at one of the Port Elizabeth clubs where I had been performing. The depression that had come over me was especially powerful that night. When I got to the club, I took some heroin and began to drink anything strong enough to numb my mind.

That's when it happened. For no earthly reason, someone walked up and stabbed me in the chest in that noisy, crowded club. I staggered to the bathroom and tried to stop the bleeding. Then, in confusion, I pushed my way out into the street.

Is this how it is going to end? I wondered. *Is my life over?*

Suddenly the words of that Anglican minister arose from deep within my spirit. I was only 10 when he visited me in my hospital room, but I could still hear the sound of his voice.

"Jesus still walks the streets today, and one day you are going to need Him. If you call on Him, He'll walk over to you, and He will touch you." Those words to me had been prophetic—though it would be several years before I even understood what the word *prophetic* meant.

Now, lying helpless in a gutter, I said to myself, *The only hope I have is Jesus.* I was bleeding very badly, and in my despair, I said, "Jesus, if You are still walking the streets, come over to me now." And He did.

At that precise moment a man walked by who knew Jesus. This young man in his late twenties became the hands of God and the voice of God extended to me. He was a total stranger, but he picked me up off the ground, carried me to his car, and drove me to the hospital.

They stitched me up, but I don't remember anything that happened during those next three days. When I "came to," the compassionate stranger was sitting in the room, waiting for me. I was released from the hospital, and he drove me to my home in Uitenhage.

When we arrived at the house, I was still in terrible pain and wanted to take more drugs. I was having withdrawal symptoms because of the three days of going cold turkey at the hospital.

It was then that he said to me, "I want to tell you about my best friend. His name is Jesus."

For the next few hours he revealed God's wonderful plan of salvation to me. Never before had I heard a story like that. I didn't argue with him or question his claims. Instead I drank in every word like a thirsty child. He didn't say, "Kim, you need to come to church and get saved." He spoke the words, "Jesus is here right now. He wants to touch you."

"What do I need to do to know Jesus?" I asked.

He led me in the "sinner's prayer," and I gave my heart to the Lord. Without question it was the most incredible thing that had ever happened to me. The weight of a lifetime was immediately lifted from me.

I wish I could tell you that this man became my lifelong friend and led me in the ways of the Lord. But that is not what happened. Instead, he was like an angel of mercy who visited my life and was gone. He didn't even return to follow up on his new convert.

A friend of mine, Manie Human, did tell me where I should go to church. "You need to come with me to the Full Gospel Church of God. That's the only place you should go."

Since he seemed so sure about it, I asked, "What kind of church is that?"

"Oh, they clap their hands and sing with excitement over there," he said.

As a rock musician, I was enticed. But I wanted to know more. "Is it an English church?"

"No," he said, "it's Afrikaans."

You must understand that all my life I had been opposed to attending church. And an *Afrikaans* church? That would have been totally out of the question. But not now. I couldn't wait to get there.

WILD AND TEASED

The next Sunday morning, in December 1973, I put on the only suit I owned—it was a pitch-black one. Then I found my way to the church he told me about, which was only one mile from my house.

From the moment I walked into the building, people began to turn their heads and look at me. I suppose I did look a little out of place. I was extremely thin, my hair was very long—down to my shoulders—and it was wild and teased. I stood out in that ultraconservative church where the women wore their hair in buns and didn't wear jewelry or makeup.

But they seemed to tolerate me.

The church seated about 400, but there were, at most, 75 people in attendance. The congregation was mainly older folks with just a few young people. The minister was known as "Pastor Pretorius." He reminded me of an old wrestler—a big fellow with a round face and a broken nose.

The praise and worship were wonderful. They were clapping their hands and singing music I had never heard before. I did my best to follow along. Then, during the first part of the meeting, Pastor Pretorius stopped the music and said, "I feel led to change the order of this service. If anyone is here who needs to make a public confession of his sins before God, I want you to come down to the altar. We want to pray with you."

Without hesitation I walked forward and knelt at the altar. Several people gathered around me for a time of prayer, and afterward I went back to my seat. I learned later that the pastor had never before given an altar call during the early part of a service. Perhaps it was just for me.

When the meeting was over, a man in his twenties came over to meet me. "Hello. My name is Peter Frederic, and this is my wife, Leslie."

They were a friendly couple. Peter said, "I think I know where you are coming from, and I want to help you. You've been on drugs, haven't you?"

"You're right."

"Well, I can see your withdrawal symptoms," he said. "I know what is happening."

It had been only a few days since I had been off drugs, but he could see the telltale signs by the way I walked and talked.

"Can you come over to our house for lunch?" he asked.

"I'd love to."

Peter was a Mauritian, a Creole-speaking Frenchman from the island of Mauritius—about 500 miles east of Madagascar in the Indian Ocean. He had been a big drug pusher who smuggled illegal substances from his homeland to Durban.

No one else in that church could have handled so ably the complex problem I was going through at that time. The others didn't know anything about druggies or *muzos*, which is the local term for musicians.

It was during one of his trips to Durban that Peter had been wonderfully saved. He and his wife then came to visit his sister who lived in Uitenhage and decided to start a business there. That was only a month before I gave my heart to the Lord. I believe the Lord brought Peter to my town because He knew that I would need such a person.

Seated in his living room, Peter began to pray over me for deliverance because he knew what kinds of things I had been through. The suffering I had experienced was dreadful. The pain was deeper than people will ever know.

Peter Frederic placed a high priority on the power of confession. All that afternoon he kept asking, "What have you done in your life that you need forgiveness for? Go ahead and speak it out."

When I would name something, he would immediately pray that it would be removed forever. Then he'd inquire, "What is it that you are hiding? Try to remember it and vocalize it. You've got to empty yourself of it." Then we would pray again.

Never had I been so open and honest with anyone else in my life. But instead of feeling shame for what I had done, I felt as if my life was being totally cleansed.

"I believe you are ready to be filled with the Holy Spirit," he said at last.

"What is that?" I wanted to know.

He did his best to tell me what happened on the day of Pentecost and how it is still happening today. Then he said, "Oh, it's too hard to explain. But you'll understand when you receive Him."

We began to pray out loud, and suddenly, something like an otherworldly tidal wave hit me. There in his home I was filled with the Holy Spirit and began shouting and rejoicing. I spoke in an unknown tongue for several hours. It was as if I was being immersed in fire and rain at the same time. Even the tips of my fingers and toes were tingling with a power I had never felt before.

You've Gone Crazy

Later that night I came bouncing into my house like someone from another planet. I was so filled with the Spirit that I was still screaming and shouting for joy. My parents were both home, and I could see the looks of absolute horror on their faces.

"Let me tell you what has happened to me," I said. "I've met Jesus. And I've been filled with the Holy Spirit."

They just stared at me.

"No more music, no more rock bands, no more movies," I told them. "I'm giving the whole lot up. It is finished."

It was as if there had been a death in the family.

"You're off your head. You've gone crazy" was their response. My mother specifically was very angry with me because I was giving up my music career. She placed a higher priority on social lifestyle than on religion. Up to that point, my music had been one of the major bragging points in her life.

No one in our family had ever had such a religious experience. I was the first person in an entire generation who had found salvation through Christ in such a way.

For the next several months a total breakdown in communication occurred between my parents and me. Even though I continued to live at home, they did not want to discuss my religious experience. They treated me like a stranger.

But my salvation was real. The good money I had been making in music now seemed meaningless. That week I wrote letters to my rock band and to the movie producer to tell them I was finished with that part of my life.

However, I couldn't seem to escape the contract with the band. I went to my new friend Peter, and said, "I can't play rock music anymore—not even one more show."

When I called the band manager, he said, "There is no escape clause. You'll either fulfill this contract, or I will have to take legal action against you."

That difficult situation provided the opportunity for me to pray one of my first prayers as a new Christian. "Lord, please help me to be released from this contract. I don't want to go back into that life."

On Friday night I was supposed to be at the club. But something amazing happened. That Friday afternoon I received a call saying that several other members of the band had been rushed to the hospital with food poisoning. The gig was canceled along with the contract! That was my final weekend in the rock music business.

I HEARD A VOICE

With the pressure at home, I couldn't wait for Sunday morning to come so I could return to the "happy, clappy" church. I walked through the door with a big smile on my face; I wasn't prepared for the reception I was about to receive. A burly deacon who had a deep scowl on his face greeted me. Instead of giving me a warm handshake, he grabbed me by the arm and literally threw me out of the building. "We don't want your kind back here at all," he shouted.

I began to walk away, confused and angry. But my friend Peter saw what was happening and came running after me. "Don't worry about him," he said. "It's just that the way you dress and the way you wear your hair is too radical for him. He can't handle it."

"I'm not sure I belong here," I said with great disappointment.

"Don't give up now," Peter said. "Just go and cut your hair."

I managed a little smile and said, "Peter, you are talking about something very sacred now. I can make a lot of changes, but don't ask me to cut my hair."

"No, Kim," Peter disagreed. "If you want to learn about Jesus in this church, you need to cut your hair. There is no use offending these people."

"Peter," I argued, "you are asking me to give up my life. It has taken me *years* to grow my hair this long."

The next day I went to my sister-in-law Vanessa and said, "Start cutting! I want it really short." And that's what she did. When I returned to the church the next Sunday, the people at the door said, "Welcome. Is this your first visit?" They didn't even recognize me.

After a few weeks the pastor came to me and said, "Kim, you need to be baptized in water. That's what the Bible says you should do after being saved."

The baptismal service was on January 1, 1974, and it seems like only yesterday. What a service! The word had spread among my bewildered friends that something had happened to me. "He's flipped. We've got to go and check this out." At every church meeting more and more of my old pals showed up. The night of my baptism more than 150 young people came from all over the region. Motorcycles lined the street, and people in the neighborhood were bewildered.

The visitors looked rather scruffy. The deacon who had once thrown me out was overwhelmed, so he tried to keep them out. I had to plead for their cause. "How are we ever going to see these people saved? We've got to let them in!"

The deacons decided to separate my friends from the rest of the congregation and let them all sit in the balcony. It was like a spiritual apartheid, but it was better than nothing.

When the time came for me to be baptized, Pastor Pretorius prayed over me and said, "In the name of the Father, the Son, and the Holy Ghost," and he put me under the water. I was immersed from my feet to the top of my short hair. The moment I came out of the water I heard a voice that I had never heard before. It was speaking to me as clearly as anything I had ever heard. It was God's voice.

How did I know it was the Lord speaking? Let me tell you, when God speaks, you won't have to wonder. You'll just know.

The Lord said two distinct things to me. First He said, "I am calling you to be a minister of the gospel."

The minute I heard those words, I shouted out from the baptismal tank. "God's called me! God's called me to be a minister!"

I'm sure the preacher felt like putting me back under the water.

Then God spoke again and gave me an incredible prophetic word. He said, "None of your household will go to the grave without salvation."

That night many of my friends found Christ as their Savior. But what about my mother and father? What about my brothers and sister? Had I really heard from God?

 CHAPTER TWO

WAITING IN THE HALLWAY

"I know you think you've been called to preach, but I don't believe it," said Pastor Pretorius. I had only been a Christian for a few weeks, and he was already giving me a stern lecture.

"Here's what we want you to do," he said forcefully. "We want you to sit in this church for at least three years—no music ministry, no preaching, no nothing!"

Then he got to the core of the matter. "If you are prepared to be faithful to this church and hear what God has to say, we will build your character and drive this rebellion out of you."

Things were happening so fast in my life that I hardly knew how to respond. In just over a month I had been stabbed, saved, sent to church, filled with the Spirit, rejected by my family, freed from drugs, kicked out of church, baptized in water, and spoken to by God. Now I was being grounded! What next?

"Pastor," I said, "you know what is best for my life. God brought me here for a purpose, and I am ready to learn."

That church provided exactly what I needed most: discipline. Most pastors would have brought me to the platform and let me use my talent for the Lord. But not here. They believed I needed to sit in the pew and become a student of the Word. The church was legalistic, dogmatic, and uncompromising, but for me it was the greatest thing that could have ever happened.

Pastor Pretorius was an important influence in my life, but Peter Frederic was the one who discipled me and became my spiritual father. I shudder to think what my life would have become without his influence.

Peter and I would pray together for hours and hours—walking up and down the aisles of the church, praying in the Spirit. More than once wle entered into 40 days of fasting and prayer.

To earn a little money, I took a job as a storeman in the parts department at a Volkswagon factory. I was fortunate to have any job at all since I was a high school dropout and had no skills other than music.

During my first year as a Christian, there were only three major activities in my life: working, praying, and studying God's Word. Every time the doors of the church were open, I was there. Peter and I continued our daily prayer meetings, and my understanding of God's Spirit grew like a tree planted in good soil.

GONE "BONKERS"

At home the tension grew worse. At first my parents would not speak to me about my experience with Jesus. Even when we would talk, we had nothing in common. I had become one of those "strict" Christians. I wouldn't go to the movies. I wouldn't listen to rock music. I only wanted to be in the presence of the Lord—and my parents didn't.

One night a hypnotist came to our town to put on a show. My parents said, "Kim, come see the show with us."

"No," I told them. "That is not of the Lord."

They couldn't understand.

The pastor would not allow me to play the piano publicly, but I felt a tremendous need to release the music that was inside me. Every chance I had, I came home, closed the door of my room, and turned on my keyboard. It was there I would worship the Lord with music. For hours I would become lost in the

Spirit, singing the songs of the Lord. I can understand how my parents thought I had gone "bonkers" when they heard all that noise coming out of my room.

During that time I developed a deep relationship with God, and He began to flow through me with what I now know as a prophetic anointing.

How did I know my conversion was real? Never in my life had I developed a passion for anything that compared to my love for God. The pull was more powerful than rock music, more potent than any drug, and stronger than the lure of the world. Nothing could compare with the anointing of God's Spirit. It was pure heaven.

At the end of that year Peter gave me some devastating news. "Leslie and I are moving back to Durban." It broke my heart because he was the only one who really encouraged me. Other members of the church didn't see the same potential in me. Suddenly, I was alone, without a friend.

When he left, I went to the pastor and told him I would do anything possible to serve the church. I thought he might say, "Kim, I believe the time has come for you to lead worship," or "Would you be interested in teaching a Sunday school class?"

Instead he asked if I could help clean the building each week. "Of course I will" was my response. I began my ministry of sweeping the sanctuary, washing the windows, and cleaning the commodes.

I left my job at the factory and started to work as a salesman. I never thought of a career, however. The message of the church was that the Lord's return was so imminent that we should not concern ourselves with earthly pursuits or ambitions. I didn't argue with that application of Scripture—or with anything else that was unique to the church. I knew that God had planted me there for a purpose, and I was determined to learn what it was.

WAITING IN THE HALLWAY

During my second year as a Christian, I went to Pastor Pretorius and said, "Pastor, I feel that I am ready to attend Bible college and would like you to help me get in."

"I don't believe you are called to the ministry," he replied. "But I'll arrange for you to meet with some of the church officials."

We drove to the headquarters of the denomination in Pretoria, the capital city of South Africa. It was more than 600 miles from Uitenhage. After my interview, I waited in the hallway for nearly three hours while they discussed my potential and finished their other business. Finally, one of the men came out and said, "I know you won't like to hear this, but, young man, we don't believe you are cut out to become a minister."

During my third year at that church I decided to try again. "Please, pastor," I said, "can't you convince the officials that I need to be in Bible school? I know God has called me."

Once again we traveled to the church headquarters. I prepared for the interview by asking the pastor everything I could about doctrine and theology. I also got a fresh haircut and put on my most conservative clothes.

This time Pastor Pretorius said, "Gentlemen, this is a good man. I've never been convinced that he should be a minister, but he thinks God has called him. Why don't you give him a chance?"

The denominational leaders questioned my position on everything from eternal security to Pentecostal manifestations. And I thought I gave the right answers. After a rather lengthy exchange, they said, "We'd like you to wait outside."

When they had made a decision, they came out to me and said, "Kim, we know you love the Lord, but we're still persuaded that you will never become a pastor or an evangelist. You would just be wasting your time pursuing it." Rather they suggested that I play the church organ.

I was distraught. When I returned home, I fell on my face before God and cried out: "Lord, is it over? Have I spent three years here for nothing? Didn't I hear Your voice when I was baptized? Didn't You call me to the ministry?"

Not knowing where else to turn for help, I sat down one day and did something quite unusual. I handwrote a letter to Oral Roberts in Tulsa, Oklahoma. I had read his book *Seed Faith*, and I believed he could help me.

"Dear Mr. Roberts," I began, "my name is Kim Clement. God has called me to the ministry, and I am asking for your help. Twice the board of a denominational Bible college has rejected me. My pastor has even told me that I am not truly called, and you may feel the same way. However, I want you to pray about my request. I need to study and prepare myself for what God has planned for my life. I have no way of attending a Bible college, and I cannot afford it. I would appreciate any help or direction you can give me."

With the letter I enclosed a cash gift of five *rand*—or about two dollars.

About one month later I received boxes and boxes of books from the theology department of Oral Roberts University— textbooks, Bible handbooks, commentaries, workbooks, and inspirational volumes. I couldn't believe it!

Every day I spent hours devouring the pages of those marvelous books. I could now identify things I had experienced and say, "That happened to me!" or "I didn't know that was in the Bible!"

Oral Roberts had planted a seed in me, and those books confirmed my call and enlarged my vision and broke the curse of poverty and stinginess that had held our family in bondage for decades.

MIRACLE ON THE MONUMENT

One night I was awakened from my sleep at about two o'clock in the morning. It was as if the Lord had tapped me on the shoulder. "Go up to the monument and pray," I heard Him say in my spirit.

I walked over to the window and saw that rain was pouring down outside. "Are you sure, Lord?" I asked.

But then I was wide-awake, and I sensed urgency about what God was telling me to do. I put on my raincoat and began to walk up the hill. It was the same park I had escaped to when I was taking drugs and skipping school a few years earlier.

The hill is quite steep. Just in front of the monument to King George V is a fence with an iron gate. That night the gate was locked, and I wasn't sure what to do. I said, "Lord, didn't You ask me to go up to the monument and pray? Well, that's where I'm headed." And I climbed over the fence.

When I cleared the fence and dropped back on the ground, I sensed the presence of the Lord in such an awesome way that I began to cry. As I followed the lighted path to the top of the hill, the Lord seemed so close that I could reach out and touch Him. I was praying out loud and conversing with Him.

As the rain continued to fall, I reached the top of the hill and was about to walk up the steps to the monument.

Suddenly, I heard a loud commotion coming from the direction of the gate. As I turned around, I saw two huge men running toward me. *Lord, You haven't brought me here to kill me now, have You?* I thought in panic.

When the men came closer I could see they were uniformed guards and had police batons in their hands. They stopped me and said, "Do you have any identification? We are security police."

I was so startled I hardly knew what to say.

"What are you doing here?" they wanted to know. "Didn't you see that the fence was locked? We've had drug dealing here, and we want to know what you're up to."

"I'm actually doing nothing," I said, as I stood there in the rain. "I'm just praying."

They continued questioning. "Mister, we will let you go if you can tell us where the person is who was walking up the hill with you."

"Listen," I said. "I promise you there was no one else but me. I just wanted to come up here and pray."

Both of them were adamant. "Look, we saw two of you walking up this pathway, and we are going to find the other man."

By this time I was getting curious. "What did the other man look like?" I asked.

"He was slightly taller than you. We saw the two of you talking while you walked up this hill," said one of the policemen. "Don't move. Stay right here. We're going to find him."

For nearly 30 minutes they searched the entire area and could find no one. When they returned I said, "Look, fellows, I know this sounds crazy, but that was Jesus you saw."

I returned home soaking wet but praising God. I realized this was a proof that the Lord was with me every step of the way.

THE BIG CONCERT

I knew it would be futile to wait another year and knock on the door of the denomination once again. I met with the pastor and said, "At least let me go out and perform a concert. That's something I know how to do. I believe it could really minister to people."

For three years I had obeyed the Lord, the church, and those He had placed in my life. And more than once I had recalled those early words of the pastor telling me that if I would be faithful, "We will build your character and drive this rebellion out of you."

That is what happened. My defiance of authority had been replaced with a deep love for the Word and for worship. I thought, *Perhaps this church has been the Bible college I needed.*

The church had experienced some changes along with me. Instead of a congregation of 75, it was now filled to its capacity of 400. People were driving in from all over the region. It was quite phenomenal.

The more I thought about it, the more I realized how vital it had been to be "rejected" from active ministry. I recalled how the disciples spent three years at the feet of Jesus before they were released to do His work.

Pastor Pretorius finally answered, "Kim, you are right. I think the time has come. I'm all in favor of your doing a concert, and we will sponsor it."

I found a neutral auditorium where young people from the city would feel comfortable. Several of my old band members had now been saved, and we began practicing together. The songs were patterned after those of Andrae Crouch, who influenced my music tremendously. As we practiced for the concert, I thought, *Wouldn't it be something if I became the white Andrae Crouch?*

Oh, what a difference it was to be playing music for the Lord! We printed hundreds of handbills and flyers announcing Kim Clement and the Righteous Judeans. There were eight of us in the band.

When I entered the auditorium that night, I was shocked by the size of the crowd. The place was packed simply through word of mouth. The news had spread through the rock crowd: "Kim is back into music. He's doing a concert!"

Just before walking onto that stage, I couldn't help but think that it was the beginning of my music ministry. Everything was planned. We had rehearsed 12 songs, and I could almost envision the standing ovation we would receive when the night was over.

It was a mixed crowd—half were Christians and half were unbelievers. The sound system was powerful. The lighting effects were superb, and everything ran smoothly for the first two or three songs. Then the event turned into total *chaos*.

Something happened to me that I never could have planned or expected. I abandoned the prepared program and began singing the "song of the Lord" under a heavy anointing. It was *His* song, His melody, and His words—not something I had rehearsed.

I was so used to ministering *to* Him that when it came to entertainment, I couldn't do it anymore. I just started flowing in God's Spirit, and He took over the meeting. The band members were in total shock and so was I.

While I was worshiping the Lord at the piano, people were being "slain in the Spirit." Some were lying on the floor; some were worshiping God in a heavenly language. Teens were coming to the edge of the stage for salvation. At one point, I jumped off the platform and started praying for people. They were coming forward, and all heaven broke loose. It was a wonderful mess.

Then I began to prophesy. God was giving me words for the people, and I delivered them—giving specific words to specific people.

I glanced over at Pastor Pretorius and the leaders from our church, and their eyes were as big as saucers. I could only wonder what they thought. Well, I didn't understand it myself. I thought we would play our songs and have the crowd cheering. And when I would say, "Good night, and God bless you," they would clap for more. But that's not how it turned out.

It was clear that God was moving in my life. But a concert ministry? It was doubtful that would ever happen.

"THAT'S AN ORDER!"

The next invitation I received was not from a church. It was a call for duty in the South African army. It wasn't totally unexpected since every young man was required to do a stint in military service. So when I was 21 years old, I was stationed at a camp near the town of Bethlehem in Orange Free State.

It was a great experience because I went as a Christian and viewed it as an opportunity to serve the Lord. Physically, it was demanding. Spiritually, however, it was much tougher than I imagined.

In my off hours I played the piano for some coffeehouse ministries, and the word got around that I was a fair musician. That's when a high-ranking officer called me and said, "Mr. Clement, we have assigned you to play for a dance at the officers' club next Saturday night."

I was stunned. "No, sir," I said. "I don't play that kind of music."

The officer wasn't used to a new recruit saying no. He let me know that I had refused an order, and the next thing I knew I was sent out to "the hill" with my backpack. I was required to run the terrain for three or four hours.

The next time I refused to play, the punishment was even harsher. When I was on the ground doing military exercises, the drill sergeant kicked me and broke one of my ribs.

A few days later an army major came to my bunkhouse and said, "Mr. Clement, you will be playing at the officers' club this weekend. That's a direct order."

He meant business. "I will play on one condition," I bargained.

"What's that?"

"That you allow me to play Christian music."

"We can't dance to religious tunes," he huffed.

"Well, I'll show you that you can," I responded with confidence.

That Saturday night I hardly knew what to expect. The club was packed with officers and their decked-out guests. They were definitely in a party mood. When it was time to play, I went to the piano and began with all the up-tempo songs I could think of. They were dancing to the rhythm of "This Is the Day That the Lord Has Made," "The Lord Lives," and "Blessed Be the Rock."

They'd be shocked if they knew the words to these songs, I thought with a smile. Later in the evening I slowed the tempo down and began to play the beautiful melody of my favorite worship chorus, "Alleluia."

I closed my eyes and prayed that somehow the Lord would flow through my fingers, through the keyboard, through the strings of that piano, and into their hearts.

By the time I had played it the third or fourth time, I could actually feel the Spirit of God enter that room. The loud noise of drinking and dancing had changed into an atmosphere that I could not explain.

"What is that song you are playing?" whispered one of the officers as he came over to the piano. I could see the tears welling up in his eyes.

"It's a song called 'Alleluia,'" I said as I continued to play.

Another officer joined him, and they began asking questions about my background. I told them how Christ had radically transformed my life. Before the evening was over, I was able to pray with both of them and lead them to the Lord. One of them, Major Ivan Graham, then became a wonderful friend.

VITAL LINK

When I came out of military service about a year later, I was still at a crossroads regarding God's direction for my future. The only thing I could cling to was the clear voice I had heard when I was baptized. I knew in my heart that God had called me to the ministry.

I decided not to go back to the Full Gospel Church of God. Without question my three years there had been ordained by the Lord, but I knew that if I returned, I would once again be locked in with no way to express God's call.

It was rare for pastors to invite me to preach because they didn't understand where the Lord was leading me. They knew what to expect from an evangelist or a teacher, but not from someone with a prophetic ministry. Instead of an outlined sermon with three points and a conclusion, God gave me revelations, and I would share them. Most pastors just couldn't relate to that.

I found a job at a music store in Port Elizabeth, demonstrating and selling pianos, synthesizers, and various instruments. At night I was involved in street evangelism in a Christian coffeehouse called "The Vital Link." It was an effective ministry to prostitutes, drug addicts, and young people who were searching for answers.

One day the phone rang. "Hello. Is this Kim Clement?" asked the voice at the other end of the phone. I was at my office in the music store.

"Yes, it is," I replied. "How can I help you?"

"My name is Pastor Jimmy Crompton," he said. "I am the pastor of the Pentecostal Protestant Church here in Port Elizabeth. God has told me that you are to join my staff as a minister."

I said, "I don't know you. But do you realize that I have no credentials whatsoever? In fact, I never even finished high school."

"I'm not worried about that at all," he replied. "God told me that you are to come and be our music director and youth pastor."

We arranged to meet at the church, and I knew immediately it was where the Lord wanted me. It was a growing church of about 300, and Jimmy Crompton came from a great spiritual heritage. His father had traveled with the remarkable British evangelist Smith Wigglesworth.

As a minister of the Word, I left much to be desired, but Jimmy made me feel I was something special in the Kingdom of God. He allowed me to express all the things the Lord was giving me, and I was encouraged to be sensitive to the moving of the Holy Spirit in every service. During the times of praise and worship, a mighty anointing would fill the sanctuary, and the entire congregation would begin singing the song of the Lord. Pastor Crompton also had an understanding of prophetic gifts, and he permitted me to use them. What a major role he played in the early stages of my ministry!

A few months after joining the church staff, I was invited to play the piano for a meeting of the local Full Gospel Businessmen's Fellowship. The guest speaker was Fred Roberts, a well-known pastor from Durban. While I was playing the piano during the early part of the service, I began to lead people in some praise choruses. Over 500 people lifted their hands and began to worship the Lord. Then Fred Roberts walked over to me and said, "God told me that it's your meeting."

I was startled and told him, "But you don't understand. I'm not a preacher!"

He repeated it again. "It's your meeting. Go for it!" Then he walked back to his seat.

Never before had I been asked to minister to an audience that large. But there was no time to become nervous or afraid. God was present, and I began singing in the Spirit and prophesying—in short, just being God's voice. I preached for about 25 minutes and, to my amazement, the altar was lined with people coming to find Christ.

I'm not sure what happened in the lives of those who attended that meeting, but I certainly know what God did for me. If I ever needed a confirmation of God's call, that was it.

Each time after that when Fred Roberts came to our area to speak, he would call me to lead the music. It was obvious that our ministries flowed together in an unusual way. "I'd love for you to come to Durban sometime," he told me. "You have an open invitation."

Romance—Love

Since the moment of my conversion I had not become romantically involved with anyone. It wasn't by chance. The

Lord clearly told me that I was not to spend my time looking for a future wife—or even to date. I was so in love with Christ that I didn't care about relationships anyway. He said, "Concentrate on Me. I will bring someone to you, and you will know she is the one when you see her."

One night at the church in Port Elizabeth, a young lady walked through the door. Her name was Jane Barnes. She was from a British family in Durban and had traveled to our city to visit a girlfriend who attended our church. Even though she had been raised in a Christian home, she was not living for the Lord. But that night something glorious happened. She rededicated her life to the Lord.

After the service, something else took place. We were introduced to each other. The moment I met her, I said to myself, *This is the one! This is the girl I am going to marry!* I didn't know it at the time, but she was the niece of Fred Roberts.

Jane and I fell deeply in love, and we kept the phone lines busy. I thought I was going to have to get a part-time job to pay for the calls!

A few weeks later I took a weekend off from my duties to visit her in Durban. While I was there, Fred Roberts was conducting a retreat outside the city, so we drove out to see him.

During one of the services a prophetic word was given to me for the second time in my life. The first was at the church in Uitenhage when a visiting minister prayed over me and said, "All I want to say to you, sir, is that God has called you to the ministry." Not even Pastor Pretorius was fully convinced of that, but I claimed those words as from the Lord. Now, at the retreat, God gave me another prophetic word. Someone prayed for me and said, "God is going to move you to Durban."

At first I ignored the word, but it gradually began to witness to my spirit. After I returned to Port Elizabeth, every time I closed my eyes, those words kept coming back. I finally told Pastor

Crompton about it, and he said, "If that is what the Lord has planned, I won't stand in your way."

It proved to be the greatest move of my life. Not only did I join the staff of Fred Roberts' church, but a short time later Jane and I were married.

COMMUNION THEN DOMINION

I had only been in Durban for two months when Pastor Roberts called me and the other associate pastor into his office. "God has clearly told me that the racial barriers of ministry must be broken. Spiritually, there must be communion before there can be dominion."

That ran contrary to the rules of the Pentecostal fellowship to which the church belonged. Their policy was to obey the laws of the land. They did not allow blacks in their churches.

Pastor Roberts continued, "I believe we should resign from the denomination, go into the heart of the city, and defy the apartheid laws. We should open our doors to every nationality."

It was a huge decision, since he had been at the church for many years, and the congregation had grown to several hundred. But it was the right decision.

In 1979, they purchased the Lyric Theater in downtown Durban and opened the doors of the Durban Christian Center. Only a handful attended the first service. Within a few months that handful grew to more than 2,000—Zulus, Xhosas, Bantus, Indians, coloreds, English, Afrikaners—a rainbow of God's people.

Fred Roberts became a mentor to me, and he took great delight in seeing my prophetic ministry grow. His son-in-law, Neville Macdonald, and his daughter, Wendy, were also associate ministers and a vital part of the team. Neville later began a multi-racial church in Cape Town, which grew to be the largest congregation in that city.

God was doing marvelous things in the meetings at Durban, and I began to receive invitations from Europe, Australia, and the United States. Today the church has a membership of over 20,000.

In 1986, I was traveling in Canada with my family and was scheduled to minister in the United States. One morning I rushed into the airport to pick up my tickets on American Airlines. The woman at the counter said, "Mr. Clement?" She had a concerned look on her face.

"Yes," I replied. "Is there some kind of a problem?"

"I have been asked to give you this message: Your father has died in South Africa."

My heart sank. Then, in a fraction of a second, the Lord said, "Do you remember My Word?" My mind flashed back to the voice of God I had heard when I was baptized: "None of your household will go to the grave without salvation." But my father had not been in a right relationship with Christ. I was bewildered.

There in the airport lobby I spoke out loud and told the clerk, "It's impossible! The Lord told me he is not going to die. He's not saved or filled with the Spirit yet."

She had a puzzled look on her face. "Well, I don't know anything about that," she said, "but this is the message I was told to give you. I'm very sorry."

As you'll read later, the word that the Lord gave me at my baptism came to pass, though not in the way I expected.

 CHAPTER THREE

BECOMING THE VOICE

My life has been filled with surprises.

As a child I expected to become a classical pianist, but that's not what happened. I was on my way to becoming a rock superstar when Jesus came into my life. I dreamed about studying for the ministry, but the Bible college wouldn't admit me. Even when I believed I had found my calling as a professional Christian musician and presented my first Christian concert, I was able to sing only three songs.

I felt like Jacob, who fell in love with Laban's daughter Rachel. Jacob told Laban, "I will serve you seven years for Rachel your younger daughter" (Gen. 29:18). He endured many hardships during his wait. But on his wedding night, when Jacob lifted his bride's veil, he found Leah, Laban's firstborn daughter, instead of Rachel.

So often, that is how God works.

During my years "in the desert" at the church in Uitenhage, God stirred something within me that I hadn't sought after and didn't understand. Yet it was there. After being rebuffed and rejected at every turn, I prayed for a word from the Lord about it. At first, I heard only a still, small voice—just a whisper—"I have called you to be a prophet to many nations."

"A *prophet?*" I asked the Lord. "You want me to be a prophet?"

I hardly knew how to define the word, but every time I prayed, the voice grew louder and louder. Finally, with great force, God declared, "I have called you to be a prophet to many nations."

I opened my Bible and read about the specific ministries God gives to the church. "And He Himself gave some to be apostles, some prophets, some evangelists, and some pastors and teachers" (Eph. 4:11). These are called the fivefold ministries.

As I looked around, I saw apostles who provided spiritual leadership, pastors who proclaimed the Word, evangelists who preached to the unsaved, and teachers who built up the Body of Christ. But where were the prophets?

One person told me that I should read about them in the Old Testament—great prophets like Ezekiel, Daniel, Hosea, and Joel.

"No, I am reading the *New* Testament," I told him. "It says there are to be prophets in the church."

It Can't Be Taught

Please understand that I had no desire to become a prophet. The term itself often makes people think that someone is self-appointed and attempting to gain stature in the church. Instead, it was God's specific calling on my life.

But God is raising up prophets today in unprecedented numbers throughout the world, and you will surely come under the sound of their voices. The Lord may use a prophet to speak directly to you. That's why it is so important to understand the ministry of the prophet today.

If you think this book is going to tell about the dramatic exploits of a prophet who travels the globe telling people about their lives, you will be disappointed. Instead, this book is about *you.* I firmly believe that God desires that the voice of God flows to and through *you*. I want you to be prepared when God calls *you* to become His voice.

On these pages we will be examining questions including:

- What is the primary purpose of prophecy?
- Why is God raising up prophets in this generation?
- Is His voice still speaking to us?
- Why are so few people actually receiving the promise of God? (See Acts 2:17-18.)
- Is prophecy for the Church, for the world, or for both?
- How can we know God's voice?
- How can we identify a false prophet?
- Does every prophecy have to come true?

When I accepted God's unique call on my life, I began to imagine the great things that God was going to do using this gift. I could actually "see" them. I could visualize myself speaking such truth to people that they would find repentance. I began to dream about giving a word and seeing someone called to the ministry. I even dreamed about *singing* a prophetic utterance that would bring people out of wheelchairs and out of beds of affliction. Then God tugged at my sleeve. It was time to exercise my gift.

Do you remember what happened to Joseph while he was in prison? God gave him the gift of interpreting dreams, but before he approached the Pharaoh, Joseph exercised his prophetic unction on the Pharaoh's chief butler and chief baker. Joseph interpreted each man's dream, and God's word through Joseph came to pass within three years. Two years later Pharaoh had a dream and sent for the young Hebrew. He told Joseph,

> *I have had a dream, and there is no one who can interpret it. But I have heard it said of you that you could understand a dream, to interpret **it** (Genesis 41:15).*

Joseph explained that it wasn't *his* power, but God's—*God* would provide the answer. Not only did Joseph become the voice of the Lord, but also he was released from prison. The king said, "See, I have set you over all the land of Egypt" (Gen. 41:41).

As I began to exercise my gift, God's voice became clearer and clearer. And the more I understood about prophecy, the bolder a spokesman for the Almighty I became.

A VOICE IN THE GARDEN

The voice of God is not a new phenomenon. It began at creation.

"God said, 'Let there be light'; and there was light" (Gen. 1:3). How did He create light? He *spoke* it into existence. And that is how He created the earth, vegetation, animal life, and mankind. He said it, and it happened.

God created man with His breath.

And the Lord formed man of the dust of the ground, and breathed into his nostrils the breath of life; and man became a living being (Genesis 2:7).

He *spoke* the words, "Be fruitful and multiply" (Gen. 1:28). God creates by speaking. I believe that one of the basic principles of prophecy is that God's voice creates something new in our lives. For example, He will supply us with direction, guidance, or knowledge we do not already possess.

The Lord's purpose for Adam and Eve was to give mankind dominion over the earth and fill it with righteousness. Every day, as they heard God's voice, their knowledge, wisdom, power, and abundance increased. The character of God was being formed in them. The more they heard, the more familiar His voice became to them.

God had said to Adam and Eve, "Be fruitful and multiply; fill the earth and subdue it" (Gen. 1:28). If mankind had continued to hear the voice of God, we would have been secure and creative and had dominion. But satan realized that we would overcome him some day, judge him and put him under our feet. He said, "I must stop them from hearing the voice of God."

The weapon satan formed also used the power of words. He told Adam and Eve, "If you will just partake of that tree in the midst of the garden you will be exactly like God" (see Gen. 3:4-5). He tempted them to disobey God, realizing that if he could cause them to be disobedient they would become afraid, and the communication between God and man would stop. But even after satan lied to Eve in the Garden and they ate of the forbidden fruit, the Lord continued to speak.

> *And they heard the sound of the Lord God walking in the garden in the cool of the day, and Adam and his wife hid themselves from the presence of the Lord God among the trees of the garden* (Genesis 3:8).

How did they know it was God? By the sound of His voice!

The Lord always wants to communicate with His people. He asks us questions so we can speak together. "Then the Lord God called to Adam and said to him, 'Where are you?'" (Gen. 3:9).

Suddenly, God's voice became frightful to Adam because he had sinned. Adam said, "I heard Your voice in the garden, and I was afraid because I was naked; and I hid myself" (Gen. 3:10). For the first time, Adam became aware of his flesh, his nakedness, and his limitations.

The voice of the Almighty was no longer a delight to the ear and a joy to the heart. It was terrifying because their natures had changed from righteousness to evil. The purity of His voice caused them to be convicted of their sin. For the first time they experienced the emotions of fear, inferiority, and bitterness. Satan also had planted the seeds of pride, arrogance, and jealousy. Finally, God banished them from the Garden.

Even then, God continued to speak. When we read the first few books of the Old Testament it becomes clear that the Lord was grieved by sin, but the sound of His voice did not diminish. When Cain killed his brother, the Lord said to him, "Where is Abel your brother?" (Gen. 4:9). Cain was so convicted by his lie that he "went out from the presence of the Lord" (Gen. 4:16).

"No More!"

Man continued to be fruitful and multiply, but there were only a few righteous men with whom the Lord could communicate. When He found a God-fearing man by the name of Enoch, He literally lifted him out of the earth so they could be together.

And Enoch walked with God; and he was not, for God took him (Genesis 5:24).

In the history of mankind there have been very few like Enoch, Noah, or Abraham who would obey God's voice. Yet He continued to speak. There came a point when the children of Israel said, "No more! We cannot stand hearing His voice any longer." They begged the Almighty to stop speaking to them (see Exod. 20:19 and Heb. 12:19).

God's heart must have been broken. Can you imagine what it would be like if your child told you, "I never want to hear the sound of your voice again because it makes me so fearful"?

What happened next was a turning point in history. For the most part, God had been speaking directly to His people from the time of creation. Then, when God was about to make a covenant with Moses and the children of Israel at Mount Sinai, the Lord called Moses to the top of the mountain and delivered the commandments to him face-to-face (see Exod. 20).

But the voice of God was so powerful that the people in the camp below heard it, too. They became frightened. Moses later described the reaction of the people:

So it was, when you heard the voice from the midst of the dark-ness, while the mountain was burning with fire, that you

came near to me, all the heads of your tribes and your elders.
And you said: "Surely the Lord our God has shown us His
glory and His greatness, and we have heard His voice from
the midst of the fire. We have seen this day that God speaks
with man; yet he still lives. Now therefore, why should we die?
For this great fire will consume us; if we hear the voice of the
Lord our God anymore, then we shall die" (Deuteronomy
5:23-25).

They knew that Moses was a righteous man and would be
protected by God. But they were sinful and not compatible with
God's voice. They said:

For who is there of all flesh who has heard the voice of the liv-
ing God speaking from the midst of the fire, as we have, and
lived? You go near and hear all that the Lord our God may
say, and tell us all that the Lord our God says to you, and we
will hear and do it (Deuteronomy 5:26-27).

They no longer wanted the responsibility of hearing God's
voice. They were saying to Moses, "We don't qualify to hear that
voice. You can listen, but not us." The voice presented such a
challenge to them that their very flesh reacted negatively—it literally began to die. Instead of hearing from God directly, they
now wanted a mediator.

At that point in history God changed the way in which He
dealt with man. During the centuries that followed He no
longer spoke to man directly, but only through His priests and
prophets. The priests would speak to God on behalf of the people, and the prophets would speak to the people on behalf of
God.

Man suffered greatly because the direct line of communication had been broken. Many today believe that the rapid decline
in longevity began at that moment. Life spans shrunk from 900
years to 800, then 300, and finally what we have today.

So how did God speak to His people through prophets?

- The widow's flour and oil did not run dry "according to the word of the Lord which He spoke by Elijah" (1 Kings 17:16).
- Elisha said to the king's messenger, "Hear the word of the Lord. Thus says the Lord..." (2 Kings 7:1).
- To an unfaithful Israel, "the Lord began to speak by Hosea..." (Hos. 1:2).
- "The Lord spoke by Isaiah" to the commander of the Assyrian army (Isa. 20:2).
- The king of Persia proclaimed liberty for those in exile "that the word of the Lord by the mouth of Jeremiah might be fulfilled" (2 Chron. 36:22).

For hundreds of years God spoke to His people through prophets like Ezekiel, Daniel, Hosea, Joel, Amos, Obadiah, Jonah, Micah, Nahum, Habakkuk, Zephaniah, Haggai, Zechariah, and Malachi. To the ordinary men and women, the heavens were shut.

When a prophet would come into the city and say, "Hear the word of the Lord," the people would start to tremble. Sometimes they were so convicted that they would say, "Go away! Speak to someone else!"

In many cases the people rejected God's word because they thought it was merely the man who was speaking. The people were under a tremendous bondage and in danger of being manipulated because they had to depend on a man to hear God for them. But what else could they do? The windows of heaven had been closed.

Arrival of the Word

Then it happened. The greatest fulfillment of prophecy took place when Christ broke through the heavenlies and was born in Bethlehem. God said, "It is time for Me to send My Word to the earth."

Jesus was that Word.

In the beginning was the Word, and the Word was with God, and the Word was God....And the Word became flesh and dwelt among us, and we beheld His glory, the glory as of the only begotten of the Father, full of grace and truth (John 1:1,14).

What a momentous event! No longer would a prophet of flesh and blood be necessary for people to hear from God. Christ was the *living* Word.

The priests of the day were angry because someone had invaded their territory. They wouldn't accept John the Baptist's being the voice of God and prophesying the coming of Jesus. "Who are you?" they wanted to know (John 1:19).

John replied in the words of the prophet Isaiah,

I am "the voice of one crying in the wilderness: 'Make straight the way of the Lord'" (John 1:23).

John eventually baptized the Messiah he predicted would come. When Jesus came out of the water, something fantastic happened in the supernatural realm.

The heavens were opened to Him, and He saw the Spirit of God descending like a dove and alighting upon Him. And suddenly a voice came from heaven saying, "This is My beloved Son, in whom I am well pleased" (Matthew 3:16-17).

Jesus' baptism marked four important events: (1) The Word had come to earth; (2) the heavens were opened; (3) the Spirit descended; and (4) a voice came from heaven.

The moment God sends His word to your heart, the Spirit alights upon that word and becomes a voice. It's actually the Spirit doing it; not us. He uses our mouths to voice what the word has already said.

After that event, Jesus' words resulted in great miracles. When the seas churned, He spoke the word and said, "Peace, be still," and the waters calmed (Mark 4:39). When Lazarus had been dead for four days, Christ knew that His voice had the power to raise him. Jesus walked to the tomb and cried with a loud voice, "Lazarus, come forth!" And Lazarus came forth, alive and still wrapped in his grave clothes (see John 11:43-44). Life was restored by the power of His voice. The word can only work when it has a voice to manifest the word.

A great transformation had taken place in the world! Man's disobedience had caused sin to appear, and that led to God's speaking only through an intermediary. So satan did everything possible to make God's prophets and priests disobedient—and sometimes he was successful.

Now, the obedience of one man—Jesus Christ—opened up the heavens. God was once again speaking directly to His people.

It should not be surprising that satan led Jesus to the mount of temptation. If Christ could be made disobedient, He would become like the rest of mankind. But the Lord was faithful unto death.

[Christ] *for the joy that was set before Him endured the cross, despising the shame* (Hebrews 12:2).

Revealed From Heaven

Peter was one of the first who heard God's voice for himself.

When Jesus came into the region of Caesarea Philippi, He asked His disciples, saying, "Who do men say that I, the Son of Man, am?" So they said, "Some say John the Baptist, some Elijah, and others Jeremiah or one of the prophets." He said to them, "But who do you say that I am?" (Matthew 16:13-15).

After being raised in a culture in which people felt unqualified to hear directly from heaven, the disciples were hesitant to answer. Then Peter found enough courage to say, "You are the Christ, the Son of the living God" (Matt. 16:16). Jesus replied, "Blessed are you, Simon Bar-Jonah, for flesh and blood has not revealed this to you, but My Father who is in heaven" (Matt. 16:17).

Because Peter had entered into a dimension of divine communication with the Father, Jesus said to him,

> *On this rock I will build My church, and the gates of Hades shall not prevail against it. And I will give you the keys of the kingdom of heaven, and whatever you bind on earth will be bound in heaven, and whatever you loose on earth will be loosed in heaven* (Matthew 16:18-19).

Since Jesus Christ restored divine communication, are the heavens now open all the time? No. They can be blocked by spiritual wickedness. Thus, we have been given the power to bind or loose things on earth and in heaven in accordance with God's voice as He speaks to us.

Christ was the Word of the Father. He told His disciples, "He who has seen Me has seen the Father. ...The words that I speak to you I do not speak on My own authority; but the Father who dwells in Me does the works" (John 14:9-10).

Then Christ gave this promise: "Most assuredly, I say to you, he who believes in Me, the works that I do he will do also; and greater works than these he will do, because I go to My Father" (John 14:12).

He was saying, "I am going back to the Father, but *you* will become the voice of God." Christ was the Word of the Father, but we were to become the voice of that Word.

Later, when the Spirit descended at Pentecost, "They were all filled with the Holy Ghost, and began to speak with other tongues, as the Spirit gave them utterance" (Acts 2:4 KJV).

The Spirit breathes on the Word and gives it a voice. When Peter came out of the upper room and began to preach the gospel, he literally became the voice of God. It wasn't really Peter that was preaching; it was the Spirit bringing forth the word.

The Pharisees once asked Jesus when the Kingdom of God would come. Jesus replied,

The kingdom of God does not come with observation; nor will they say, "See here!" or "See there!" For indeed, the kingdom of God is within you (Luke 17:20-21).

Jesus was pointing out once again that a great change had taken place in the spiritual realm. No longer would God selectively communicate to chosen individuals. He would reveal His Kingdom in the heart of anyone who would believe.

An Open Door

The purpose of a prophet today is somewhat changed from the prophet's purpose in Old Testament times when they often pronounced judgment or predicted future events. Though on some occasions New Testament prophets do those things that are not their primary role.

After years of ministering the prophetic word, I have come to understand the role of prophecy for today. When the voice of the Lord speaks, it is as if a door of opportunity has been opened. The Lord often presents a message concerning how the person should live. The word reveals the desire of God's heart—what He wants for that person. But if that person refuses to walk through the door God has created for them, he or she will not see His revelation fulfilled.

Most people have no concept of how God speaks today. I cannot count the times that sincere people have asked me questions such as, Should I marry the person I am now dating? Will I get a promotion at my job? Will my mother die from the cancer in her body?

A prophet is not a diviner of future events. God uses him or her to express what He wants to say, not what someone wants to hear.

A man in Texas recently approached me and said, "Kim, would you pray for me? I need a word from God."

I felt that this man had a good relationship with the Lord, so I said, "Why should I pray for you for a word from the Lord?"

He looked startled until I explained, "You have the same access to God's throne that I have." As a child of God he could hear the voice of God as clearly as I could.

It is time for the church to realize that every Christian should become an instrument in the hands of the Lord—receiving His clear and mighty word.

You don't need a *prophet* for every decision of your life. Instead, see yourself as the voice of God. God communicates directly to His people. But He may send a prophet to confirm what He has already spoken to you in your secret place of prayer.

The Bible speaks of the two voices of God—His voice in the heavens and His voice on earth. The writer of Hebrews says, "See that you do not refuse Him who speaks. For if they did not escape who refused Him who *spoke on earth*, much more shall we not escape if we turn away from Him who *speaks from heaven*" (Heb. 12:25, emphasis added).

Today, the Lord Himself speaks to us, though He may send a prophet to confirm it as His words.

When Jesus was baptized in water at the river Jordan, the Father spoke to Him from heaven and said, "This is My beloved Son, in whom I am well pleased" (Matt. 3:17). Then, 13 chapters later, the Lord asked His disciples, "Who do you say that I am?" (Matt. 16:15). Peter answered, "You are the Christ, the Son of the living God" (Matt. 16:16).

Peter confirmed what the Father told Jesus at His baptism. That is why Jesus told the disciple, "Flesh and blood has not revealed this to you, but my Father who is in heaven" (Matt. 16:17).

The Lord desires us to become the voice of God. Christ has broken down the partition that once existed between the Father and us. The Holy Spirit has been released on the earth. Jesus "has made us kings and priests to His God and Father" (Rev. 1:6).

People constantly ask, "Kim, do you actually hear audible words when God speaks to you?" That has happened on occasions, but the vast majority of the time, He speaks to my spirit, and I have learned to recognize His voice. God certainly has the capability of speaking with an audible voice. But those who tell you they have heard "the voice of God" will almost always say that the communication has been Spirit to spirit. It is important that you learn to hear God's voice in whatever forms that communication might come.

HEARING THE WORDS OF GOD

And when the woman saw that the tree was good for food, and that it was pleasant to the eyes, and a tree to be desired to make one wise, she took of the fruit thereof, and did eat, and gave also unto her husband with her; and he did eat. And the eyes of them both were opened, and they knew that they were naked; and they sewed fig leaves together, and made themselves aprons. And they heard the voice of the Lord God walking in the garden in the cool of the day: and Adam and his wife hid themselves from the presence of the Lord God amongst the trees of the garden (Genesis 3:6-8 KJV).

Man was not created in such a way that he could *physically* comprehend or receive God's voice as the voices of other humans. But he was created to hear the voice of God, only in another way—a spiritual way. Through his spirit, Adam would be able to interact with God. However, a great tragedy happened in the Garden when Adam and Eve fell by the transgression of God's Word (overstepping the boundary that God had provided for them). As they partook of the fruit, their eyes were opened and they saw themselves naked. In that instance a great disturbance in the spiritual world happened: Darkness descended upon Adam and Eve so that their spirits were no longer alive and they were unable to hear with spiritual ears or see with spiritual eyes. Their spiritual perceptivities were damaged by their sinful actions, causing them to become blinded to the heavenly realm.

Perception is the ability to have insight and foresight. When Adam and Eve heard the "sound" of the Lord God walking in the Garden, they hid themselves. Why? Because God had become an imperceptible and unfamiliar sound to them so that they could no longer detect the clear spiritual voice of God. God's sound had become a strange sound and created fear within them.

It is our nature as human beings to run from something that is unfamiliar. We fear the unintelligible and anything else that we cannot associate with. Because of the fall, God's voice became a sound, an unclear sound, and soon God's creation lost the desire to hear that sound. I believe that the "fear factor" drove Adam from God and that same fear will prevent you from hearing God's voice. One of the first secrets to hearing God's voice is in overcoming the fear factor.

> *Then it came to pass on the third day, in the morning, that there were thunderings and lightnings, and a thick cloud on the mountain; and the sound of the trumpet was very loud, so that all the people who were in the camp trembled. And Moses brought the people out of the camp to meet with God, and they stood at the foot of the mountain. Now Mount Sinai was completely in smoke, because the Lord descended upon it in fire. Its smoke ascended like the smoke of a furnace, and the whole mountain quaked greatly. And when the blast of the trumpet sounded long and became louder and louder, Moses spoke, and God answered him by voice* (Exodus 19:16-19).

The children of Israel told Moses that they wanted him to become a mediator for them. They wanted nothing to do with high mountains, dark clouds, the smoke, and the fire. It was all too much for them. Sadly, they no longer wanted to hear God's voice personally. The voice of God was a severe sound to the children of Israel, and the same fear that gripped Adam and Eve gripped the Israelites. Adam and Eve, as well as the children of Israel, were afraid of God and hid. Adam and Eve hid in the bushes, and the children of Israel hid behind Moses. I wonder, where are you hiding?

CREATIVITY IN THE VOICE OF GOD

God said, "Let there be light," and there was light (Genesis 1:3).

God created light by His word, speaking it into existence by the power of His word. In the same manner, He created the earth, vegetation, animal life, and all of mankind. God spoke it and it happened. Whatever God said, was. One of the basic principles of prophecy is that God's voice creates something new in our lives. There is a creative power associated with His speech, and when His word comes to us it comes to us with dynamic energy. He will supply us with direction, guidance, and knowledge, all of which we do not already possess. Remember that God created man with the force of breath and words. The breath that gave them life and the words that gave them purpose were for a purpose—that mankind might have dominion over the earth and fill this earth with righteousness (God's life).

And the Lord God formed man of the dust of the ground, and breathed into his nostrils the breath of life; and man became a living being (Genesis 2:7).

God spoke these words in Genesis 1:28: "*Be fruitful and multiply.*" If He had simply breathed into him, Adam would have been a living being without a purpose or a destiny. God had to speak His *words* so that Adam would have the desire and ability to, "*Be fruitful and multiply; fill the earth and subdue it;* [and] *have dominion*" (Gen. 1:28). The words of God are dynamic sources of power that create within us the desire and the ability to fulfill His word. He gives to us the power to make the dreams come true. It is by the power of wind and word.

When the wind comes, it has to contain God's voice before any purpose can come out of it. Every day, as Adam and Eve heard God's voice, their knowledge, wisdom, power, and abundance increased. The character of God was being formed in them as they received and responded to the words of God.

If mankind had continued to hear the voice of God, we would be secure and creative beings with the ability to have dominion. Satan had to stop Adam and Eve from hearing the voice of God because he knew that eventually mankind would overcome him, judge him, and put him under their feet. If he could stop the process of communication, then the energy flow would cease.

Once Adam had fallen, the voice of God was no longer a delight to his ear or a joy to his heart. It was terrifying to him because his nature had changed from righteousness to evil.

Now, he could no longer hear His voice or recognize Him. When your hearing becomes spiritually impaired, your vision becomes confused and cloudy so that you can no longer see God's form.

RECOGNIZING HIS FORM

The process of recognizing His form will be a great challenge to you. Man does not get to choose the "form" through which God will deliver His word to you and sometimes the form will cause you to reject the words of God. Throughout the Old Testament we see that God came to man in many different forms. We have to be careful that we are not distracted by the *form* and miss the *voice.* If we are not careful we will not recognize Him in the form in which He comes to us.

Sometimes, He will come as an angel, as He came to Gideon, but sometimes He might come as an ass, as He came to Balaam. Sometimes, He will come to us as common folk, as the three men who came to Abraham. There are many forms that God can use to deliver His message to you. It will take spiritual perceptivity to recognize the voice of God in the form that He has sent to you.

Now behold, two of them were traveling that same day to a village called Emmaus, which was seven miles from Jerusalem. And they talked together of all these things which had happened. So it was, while they conversed and reasoned, that Jesus Himself drew near and went with them. But their eyes were restrained, so that they did not know Him. And He said to them, "What kind of conversation is this that you have with one another as you walk and are sad?" Then the one whose name was Cleopas answered and said to Him, "Are You the only stranger in Jerusalem, and have You not known the things which happened there in these days?" And He said to them, "What things?" So they said to Him, "The things concerning Jesus of Nazareth, who was a Prophet mighty in deed and word before God and all the people, and how the chief priests and our rulers delivered Him to be condemned to death, and crucified Him. But we were hoping that it was He who was going to redeem Israel. Indeed, besides all this, today is the third day since these things happened. Yes, and certain women of our company, who arrived at the tomb early, astonished us. When they did not find His body, they came saying that they had also seen a vision of angels who said He was alive. And certain of those who were with us went to the tomb and found it just as the women had said; but Him they did not see." Then He said to them, "O foolish ones, and slow of heart to believe in all that the prophets have spoken! Ought not the Christ to have suffered these things and to enter into His glory?" And beginning at Moses and all the Prophets, He expounded to them in all the Scriptures the things concerning Himself. Then they drew near to the village where they were going, and He indicated that He would have gone farther. But they constrained Him, saying, "Abide with us, for it is toward evening, and the day is far spent." And He went in to stay with them. Now it came to pass, as He sat at the table with them, that He took bread, blessed and broke it, and gave it to them. Then their eyes were opened and they knew Him;

and He vanished from their sight. And they said to one another, "Did not our heart burn within us while He talked with us on the road, and while He opened the Scriptures to us?" (Luke 24:13-32)

After His resurrection, Jesus appeared to many people, but they were not able to "hear" Him simply because they did not recognize Him. On the road to Emmaus, He appeared to a couple of His disciples. They had no idea who He was, and the only reason that they invited Him to continue on with them was because of His words. Blinded by their pain, they could not see that the answer to their pain was right beside them. Once their *eyes were opened* they said, "Did His words not burn in our heart?"

I don't believe that they would have been able to make this statement if their eyes were not opened to His form. The word of God must burn in your heart for it to bring about the change that is necessary. You must perceive where He is and recognize Him by divine perception. Once you see Him there will be an unveiling to your eyes and an unstopping of your ears so that His words will ever burn in your heart and have the correct effect on your life.

Stop listening and start looking. Once you find His form, you'll hear His voice. You were originally created to hear His voice—created in a unique way to hear what others cannot hear.

CREATED TO HEAR HIS VOICE

How is it possible for the Lord to speak to our inner man? Let's look at the way God created man—as a spirit being who resides in a physical body of flesh and blood. "And the Lord God formed man of the dust of the ground, and breathed into his nostrils the breath of life; and man became a living being" (Gen. 2:7). God breathed His Spirit into man so that he would become compatible with the Father. As a result, God can speak Spirit to spirit, since He has no dealings with the flesh. That is why the

Lord can speak to us spiritually, and we can understand what He is saying.

However, something more needs to happen to be able to recognize God's voice. Doing this creates an open channel between the Father and us. When you become receptive to the voice of God, you are like a soldier who has been given a great weapon. You are equipped to conquer every obstacle that comes your way.

I'm not talking about opening your Bible each morning and reading a few passages, although that is important. I'm talking about taking time for God's Word to come alive in your life—not only in your thoughts and deeds, but through your voice as well.

A FAMILIAR VOICE

The Bible says, "Let everyone who can hear, listen to what the Spirit is saying" (Rev. 2:17 TLB). Our great concern should not be how the Spirit has directed us in the past, but what the Lord is saying now.

As you continue to read these pages you will understand that God is speaking all the time. If you will take the opportunity to listen, He will do great and marvelous things in your life. You will not only receive insights about His will for your future, but He will show you how to live *now*. It is a supernatural lifestyle that the world craves but cannot attain until it turns its ears toward that wonderful sound.

When our son, Caleb, was a small baby we would put him in the nursery of the church while I conducted a service. As often happens when a child is in the presence of strangers, he would become irritated and aggravated with the other children. One night, at the end of a long gathering, I saw someone bring him into the back of the auditorium. The moment he heard the sound of my voice his entire disposition changed. He instantly was transformed from a miserable little lad into an excited child.

My voice was familiar, a sound that instinctively gave him comfort and security. He didn't need to see me or even touch me. The sound of his father's voice was all that he needed. If he could have expressed how he felt, I'm sure he would have said, "Everything's going to be all right now."

Many people believe that the glory of God is seen only through signs, wonders, and miracles, which are certainly ordained of the Lord. But I believe God's glory and greatness are revealed when He chooses to speak to you and me through the magnificent sound of His voice.

> "...when we made known unto you the power and coming of our Lord Jesus Christ, but were eyewitnesses of His majesty. For He received from God the Father honour and glory, when there came such a voice to Him from the excellent glory, This is My beloved Son, in whom I am well pleased. And this voice which came from heaven we heard, when we were with Him in the holy mount. We have also a more sure word of prophecy; whereunto ye do well that ye take heed, as unto a light that shineth in a dark place, until the day dawn, and the day star arise in your hearts" (2 Peter 1:16-19 KJV).

Some folks pray that the Lord will somehow come down from His throne and visit them. But as you serve Him, He will draw you to where He is—the holy of holies on the mount of the Lord. As a believer you have access into the heavenly realm of God.

INVADING HIS TERRITORY

The battle for the heavenlies is still being waged.

> For we do not wrestle against flesh and blood, but against principalities, against powers, against the rulers of the darkness of this age, against spiritual hosts of wickedness in the heavenly places (Ephesians 6:12).

The conflict will not end until Christ "delivers the kingdom to God the Father, when He puts an end to all rule and all authority and power" (1 Cor. 15:24). Satan will be "cast into the lake of fire and brimstone" (Rev. 20:10).

Satan, whom Scripture calls "the prince of the power of the air" (Eph. 2:2), is terrified when we become the voice of God. Our very breath has invaded his territory. That is why we need to vocalize what is in our spirits.

Jesus taught that speaking and believing go hand in hand. He said:

> *For assuredly, I say to you, whoever says to this mountain, "Be removed and be cast into the sea," and does not doubt in his heart, but believes that those things he says will be done, he will have whatever he says. Therefore I say to you, whatever things you ask when you pray, believe that you receive them, and you will have them* (Mark 11:23-24).

Why are we to speak it? Not because we need to be persuaded, nor does God need to be convinced—it is because the kingdoms of darkness need to be terrorized by the voice of Almighty God. You are the instrument of God's voice.

You may ask, "Why should God use me? I'm just an ordinary person." If you are a member of the Body of Christ and have received His Spirit, the breath of God resides in you. He has given you the ability to communicate for one great purpose. Through your vocal cords He can speak to the world. Instead of asking why God should use you, ask "What does God want me to say?"

The glory of the gospel is this: We have the Word with us. And as we will see, when the Word resides in our spirits, we can become the voice of Almighty God.

How will you respond when the Lord gives you a word? What will you do when the Spirit begins to breathe on you? Will you open your mouth and become His voice?

The moment God gives you something He wants you to say, don't hesitate. Speak it out. Suddenly the heavens will open, and satan will flee.

Always remember that Jesus is the Word, the Holy Spirit is the breath, and you are the voice of God.

CHAPTER FOUR

THE PROMISE
OF TOMORROW

"We believe that you have the word of the Lord, and we have something we want you to pray about," said the pastor from Alberta, Canada, who had phoned me.

"What is it?" I asked him.

"I don't believe we should tell you," he replied. "You just pray that God will reveal it."

I had already agreed to come to his church, and now I was wondering what kind of a situation I was walking into. All I could do was pray.

For several days before I flew to Alberta, I sought God for a special word. "Lord," I prayed, "I need to hear from You. What is the message You have for this congregation?"

Then, while I was on my face before the Lord, He spoke to my spirit and said, "There is a woman in the church who is causing tremendous discord and unrest." But God gave me more than a word. He also showed me her face.

On Sunday morning when I walked to the platform for my first service, I looked out at the audience, and there she was—the same face I had seen in prayer. The woman was seated on the fourth row at the end by the aisle. Her husband was next to her.

The pastor had just introduced me when I felt something inside say, "Do it now. Do it now!"

Please, Lord, I prayed, *these people hardly know me.*

But I obeyed the urging of the Spirit, stepped down from the platform, and walked over to the woman. "Please stand up," I said to her.

The moment I said those words an uncomfortable hush came over the congregation. Everyone was motionless—all attention was riveted on what was about to happen.

"God says that you are fearful of airplanes," I said.

"Yes, I am," the woman said as she looked over at her husband. They seemed happy that I knew.

"The Lord tells me that you are going to get on an airplane. It's a little one with two engines. And God is going to fly you over the snow, toward Alaska."

I continued delivering the message the Lord was giving me. "There has been trouble, but you have been faithful. God says, 'The time has come now, and I am going to release you from this place.'"

After the service, while I was having lunch with the pastor, he said, "Kim, you have no idea how God used you this morning."

"Tell me about it," I said.

He told me that woman and her husband were the founders of the church. Because of that, they felt like they could make decisions for everyone in the congregation—including the minister and his wife. "You'll never know the concern it has caused," he said. "We have been on the verge of resigning for several months."

A short time later I learned that the couple moved to Alaska. Yes, they flew. And when they left the church, the woman and her husband were happy.

Can you imagine what would have happened in the service in Alberta if I had said, "You know you are a bunch of trouble-makers, and you need to get out of here"?

Some people want to hear prophets like that. They are so sick of the devil that they would like to see old Ezekiel with his long robes declaring:

Now the end has come upon you, and I will send My anger against you; I will judge you according to your ways, and I will repay you for all your abominations (Ezekiel 7:3).

That is how God spoke through Old Testament prophets, but we are living in a new day. If I had vented a rebuke in anger, the woman could have easily rebelled. The church would have been torn apart, and the work of the Lord would have suffered.

I will never forget that experience because it brought into focus three important principles regarding the use of prophecy today. The Lord is still creative and can speak in any manner He chooses, but in almost every instance the following is true:

1. Prophecy is for the church.
2. Prophecy is to be given in love.
3. Prophecy presents a promise of God.

As prophets of the Lord our spirits have to be in tune with God's spirit. We have to know when and how to deliver God's word. We must always be aware of *why* we are giving a prophetic word (our motivations) and *how* we are giving a word from God (our manner).

QUICKENING VERSUS IMPULSE

Simon Peter had a divine quickening when he declared with great assurance that Christ is the Son of the living God. The word comes from heaven, bypasses his mind, and speaks out through a spiritual quickening. Revelation is like a flash of light that comes so quickly that the mind cannot take time to dissect and define that word. It is spoken before it is even fully perceived. Jesus made it clear to Peter that this truth did not come from exegetical, theological contemplation. It came to him from the heavenly Father. The truth that Peter expresses is the truth that heaven has declared, and Peter is only the instrument for heaven's declaration.

Then Jesus goes on to declare that He who lives by the quickening power of God will get the keys. What keys? He will get the keys to open up doors. He will be able to bind and loose because he has learned to be an instrument to heaven's voice. This kind of life will restrict and contradict sinful nature. Quickening contradicts sinful nature. Impulsiveness fashions it.

Now Peter is ready for the next phase of his training. There is no single experience that completes our training. Jesus begins to talk about crucifixion—His crucifixion, the crucifixion of *God's Son*. This did not fit within Peter's theology of "the Son of God." Simon had an impulsive thought: "No, no, no. This cannot be. God's sons don't die on crosses; they reign on thrones." Peter realizes that this could put his reputation and future at stake. "No, You will not be going to the cross." Impulsiveness, mixed with human thought and insistence and need, becomes an obstacle to God's purposes.

We think we need to be delivered from impatience and anger, so we try to get rid of our human nature. But actually there is a sense in which God puts it there. There is a divine aspect of that impulsive nature when it is exposed to the light of God's nature. Impulsiveness is a compelling force created out of a need. Simon had a need—a need to protect his destiny—and therefore he speaks. He thinks that he can speak under the same guise as if he is under this anointing. What happens, though, is quite different. Peter moves from the divine to the sinful aspect of impulsiveness, all under the disguise of anointing. It is frightening how easy that is.

Don't ever act out of a need for recognition. Just because you get one revelation right does not make you God. There exists within all of us that little need to be recognized and to be appreciated, but if that need becomes the controlling influence in our life it will eventually have destructive effects upon our life and ministry.

Consider this example. Remember the story of Naaman, captain of the host of the king of Syria? He had become afflicted with leprosy, the scourge of ancient times. He goes to Israel seeking his healing. Elisha sends his servant, Gehazi, to him and tells him to wash seven times in the Jordan River. Now, Elisha is an itinerant prophet. He is not a wealthy man and in fact lives by faith. This rich man could be the answer to his need. But Elisha does not minister out of his need. *When you act out of a need, it is no longer godly.*

Gehazi is of a different spirit, however, and seeks to take advantage of the situation. Impulsively, he runs after Naaman and propositions him, seeking some financial reward for the healing Naaman received. Naaman, of course, is quite eager to pay for his healing and offers him two bags of silver and two changes of clothing.

When Gehazi returns, Elisha is suspicious. He can smell the deceitful act. The leprosy that was upon Naaman was still in the atmosphere; and even though it was expelled from Naaman, it was now at Gehazi's door, and his deceitful act opened the door. What should have been a blessing for Gehazi was transformed into a curse because of his impulsive, greedy actions. He spoke out of his need rather than from his heart. God wants to teach us how to act out of eternal grace not external need. We must be motivated by the love of others, rather than the love of self.

A Word for the Church or for the World?

I am often asked, "Whom is God addressing when He gives a prophetic word? Is He speaking to the Church? Or is the message for the world?"

The prophet is primarily directed to give a word to the Body of Christ. Scripture tells us that "tongues are for a sign, not to those who believe but to unbelievers; but prophesying is not for unbelievers but for those who believe" (1 Cor. 14:22).

Yet there are times when God uses prophecy as a means of reaching the unbeliever. Paul said that if people prophesy "and an unbeliever or an uninformed person comes in, he is convinced by all, he is convicted by all. And thus the *secrets* of his heart are revealed; and so, falling down on his face, he will worship God and report that God is truly among you" (1 Cor. 14:24-25, emphasis added). We have misinterpreted the Scripture in Corinthians for so long. The word translated "secret" is *kryptos* in Greek, which means "treasure." God actually brings to light the treasures in your heart when you are in the presence of a prophetic atmosphere.

Since God speaks to unbelievers *through* believers, it is vital that we not only hear His word, but that we also speak His word. If we hear that sound from heaven but refuse to speak it—translating it into words that identify with the world and the culture of the unbeliever—then the message will never be heard on earth. Scripture warns us:

> *See that you do not refuse Him who speaks. For if they did not escape who refused Him who spoke on earth, much more shall we not escape if we turn away from Him who speaks from heaven* (Hebrews 12:25).

I believe there is another reason why the Lord declared that prophecy is for the Church. A believer will receive God's word and act upon it. But an unbeliever will often begin to revere the prophet and miss the message he brings.

A Heart of Love

The word God gives you must be spoken within the character and personality of Jesus. If not, the message will fail—no matter how accurate it is.

What is the heart and personality of Christ? It is love. He said, "A new commandment I give to you, that you love one another; as I have loved you, that you also love one another" (John 13:34).

Many times I have seen a prophet state truth so arrogantly that it is not effective. The Bible says, "A wicked messenger falls into trouble, but a faithful ambassador brings health" (Prov. 13:17).

The moment you say, "thus says the Lord," you are representing God in speech. If He gives you the word, He will also let you know how He is *feeling* about the person to whom you are speaking.

In Old Testament times, when a ruler sent a message to another land, the spokesman would make every effort to deliver it in the same tone in which it was given to him. If his master felt great sorrow, that's what the messenger would express. If the king had laughed, the ambassador would laugh too.

That same method needs to be used in prophetic ministry. When you speak the word of the Lord, deliver it in the tone you received it from the Lord! Do you remember when Moses misrepresented God's heart and mood by striking the rock to produce water? God had ordered him to speak to it: "Take the rod; you and your brother Aaron gather the congregation together. Speak to the rock before their eyes, and it will yield its water" (Num. 20:8). A word was all that was necessary.

But how can we be certain we are operating in perfect love? A prophet must be:

- Slow to suspect, quick to trust
- Slow to condemn, quick to justify
- Slow to expose, quick to shield
- Slow to reprimand, quick to forbear
- Slow to belittle, quick to appreciate
- Slow to demand, quick to give
- Slow to hinder, quick to help

- Slow to provoke, quick to conciliate
- Slow to resent, quick to forgive

I have made mistakes during the years God has used me in the ministry of prophecy—especially when I have become too emotionally involved in the situation.

Let me give you an example. God once showed me a man in the congregation who was committing adultery. Immediately I found that I was becoming furious with him. If I had marched up to him belligerently and said, "Sir, you are being unfaithful to your wife," the results would have been disastrous. His wife would have been humiliated, and he would have been angry with both God and me. The man might have stopped committing adultery, but it is doubtful that he would have repented from his heart.

The prophet doesn't have to say precisely what is going on in someone's life. The person hearing the prophecy will know what the prophet is talking about. A word from the Lord that only approaches the subject can still pierce their heart like an arrow. Scripture tells us that "the goodness of God leads you to repentance" (Rom. 2:4).

USED WATCHES

More than once I have been accused of being a "compromising" prophet because I have refused to publicly expose sin. One well-meaning man accused me by saying, "We know you have been to churches where there is sin taking place, and you have not revealed it." Hello! Sin is everywhere, and if I were just pointing out sin, I would be there all day. People know when they have sinned, and what they are looking for is a word that will lift them out of that dark place and give them courage to move toward God. Compassion, not condemnation, is the power that will change people's lives.

I responded by telling the man that God has directed me to speak truth by demonstrating the fruit of the Spirit—love, joy, peace, and gentleness—and restoration has taken place in hundreds of lives. Openly exposing sin can cause fear to enter a church and can cause hearts to become hardened. In that case, people will continue in their wicked ways. But when the spirit of a church is transformed from condemnation to love, there is repentance.

How should a prophet respond if God says, "Sam, the jeweler, is a crook. He is selling reconditioned watches and representing them as new"?

Again, the manner in which a prophet delivers the message is important. He or she could go to the jeweler and blatantly reveal the sin by saying, "You're a crook. You are selling used watches as if they were new."

That may, temporarily, stop the wrongdoing, but the jeweler's heart will not be transformed. Since God brings judgment to those who refuse to repent, you have brought trouble into his life.

How much better to say in his presence, "I know about a jeweler who sells reconditioned watches as if they were new." Expose sin gently and with love. Which is more important: being specific or producing repentance?

There are times, however, when God may direct you to confront sin in an unusual manner.

Jesus went into the temple and began to drive out those who bought and sold in the temple, and overturned the tables of the money changers (Mark 11:15).

That's how He demonstrated His love and respect for the house of God.

When you hear the voice of the Lord, respond—no matter what He tells you to do. Jesus said:

The works which the Father has given Me to finish—the very works that I do—bear witness of Me, that the Father has sent Me (John 5:36).

I will always remember a service conducted in Australia. There was a large crowd in the auditorium. On the front row was a man who had his hands raised, praising the Lord. God spoke to me and said, "That man is molesting little children. He is obsessed with pornography and is selling it."

When that was revealed to me, I thought, *How horrible. He is mixing what is profane with what is sacred.*

Suddenly, anger arose within me. Immediately I ran down and did something I had never done before. I started slapping the back of his hands with short but stinging slaps. I didn't have to say a word, though my flesh was tempting me. The man began to weep uncontrollably, and true repentance came into his life.

When Jesus talked with the woman at the well, He knew everything about her life, but He used great discretion in choosing His words.

> *Jesus said to her, "Go, call your husband, and come here." The woman answered and said, "I have no husband." Jesus said to her, "You have well said, 'I have no husband,' for you have had five husbands, and the one whom you now have is not your husband; in that you spoke truly"* (John 4:16-18).

The Lord actually complimented her for the half-truth she told. He didn't say, "You lied." Instead He said, "Well spoken, but...." Then He told her the truth that set her free.

A prophet must know more than what to say; he must know *how to say it.* Jesus said, "Behold, I send you out as sheep in the midst of wolves. Therefore be wise as serpents and harmless as doves" (Matt. 10:16). The prophetic word was never meant to beat people down and expose them to shame. It was meant to give hope and to help God's people understand that He has put eternity in their hearts because He has a destiny for their life.

Eternity Is in Your DNA

God has placed eternity in the hearts of men. Solomon described it this way. "He has made everything appropriate in its time. He has also set eternity in their heart..." (Eccles. 3:11 NASB). God has placed into the DNA structure of man the concept of eternity, the ability to conceive of life that extends from our distant past to our glorious future. There is within man the understanding that there is more to life than what he experiences in this time/space world. Eternity means the past, present, and future all wrapped up in one. The word *heart* in that verse means *DNA*. DNA carries the instructions for making all the structures and materials the body needs to function. Your DNA is the king of the molecules because it is the information package that carries hereditary information, which establishes personality and intelligence and sometimes curses. But God has removed your ancestral bondages from your DNA so you could do the exact opposite because of the blood of Jesus. So, I want you to know that you have eternity in your DNA.

Your DNA connects you to eternity, lifting you out of this dimension into the rarified air of where God lives. It is divinely put into you. That DNA construct makes you dissatisfied with everything that is temporary. It is dissatisfied with anything that is less than eternity. So, when the Bible says that God put eternity in your hearts (DNA), it means that you will never be satisfied until you connect with something eternal. Buddhists are not satisfied. The Hare Krishnas are not satisfied. In fact, no religion can satisfy because religion takes something eternal and demands that it become something temporary.

Inside of you is an eternal being. You are the warehouse of the *eternal* God. We have misunderstood what eternity means. When we speak of eternity, the first thing we do is get religious. We say, "Oh that means I'm going to live forever." We start thinking about puffy clouds and golden streets. That's not what eternity means. Oh, there is a portion of that which means you can live forever. But eternity doesn't mean only that you live forever. He has placed eternity in your heart, which means that you are connected to the eternal purposes of God. You are not a cosmic mistake, but you have been created with a nature that is able to rise above this dimension and soar into eternal places. You are part of the plan of God that was generated in His thoughts before the first ticking of time. Even though you live in a time/space world you will not pass away. There are things that are temporary and there are things that are eternal. You need to know the difference.

> *While we look not at the things which are seen, but at the things which are not seen: for the things which are seen are temporal; but the things which are not seen are eternal* (2 Corinthians 4:18 KJV).

> *So when this corruptible shall have put on incorruption, and this mortal shall have put on immortality, then shall be brought to pass the saying that is written, Death is swallowed up in victory* (1 Corinthians 15:54 KJV).

> *Being born again, not of corruptible seed, but of incorruptible, by the word of God, which liveth and abideth for ever* (1 Peter 1:23 KJV).

The Bible makes it clear that all that is temporary, corruptible, and perishable will fade away. But He has made it clear that we are not a part of that which is passing away, for we have been born again by an incorruptible seed (heavenly DNA) and we will live forever. We've got eternity in our blood.

There is an eternal being living inside of you. He is the man of destiny, but for many of you, like Lazarus, he is bound up with dead men's clothing. Only the voice of God will penetrate the tomb of death and call that eternal man to wake up and come forth. He is the new Lazarus who needs to come out. He is the Israel of God that is trapped in a Jacob body. And I want to get that Israel out. I want you to hear God's voice and know that you were born with eternal value and that your destiny is to be a part of God's ultimate plan for His creation.

There are many of you who are struggling. You know that there is this eternal existence inside of you and that you were meant for more than who you are right now. You won't release that eternal destiny until you've wrestled with God. You aren't going to get it out until you've had a good old fight. I'm talking about the real you, not what others have said you are. I'm talking about the person of destiny you were created to be.

Many of you are still living under the illusion that you will never amount to anything. You will never do anything. That is a lie, and you must wrestle with that lying spirit till it is gone and you discover the beauty of who you are and the destiny that is yours to discover and to fulfill.

ETERNITY IN HIS PROMISE

When God speaks, He gives a remarkable preview of what His people can expect. He talks about today and tomorrow, while using yesterday as a lesson. Eternity is in all three tenses as though they were one. When God chooses to speak to His people, many times He reveals His plans first to a prophet.

God has the power to do whatever He chooses, but He has given much of the responsibility to us. Whom did He ask to "be fruitful and multiply; fill the earth and subdue it; have dominion over...every living thing that moves on the earth" (Gen. 1:28)? He gave that assignment to you and me through Adam and Eve.

The prophetic ministry is a ministry of hope. It presents a divine revelation of God's dream for tomorrow. Rarely does the prophet tell you specific steps you must take to reach the goal. He simply tells you what God wants for your future and then departs.

It is left to the pastor or the teacher to tell you, "This is what you must do to reach that objective."

As a spokesman for the Lord I have been given a wonderful assignment. I deliver God's good news and then go on my way. Some people have the image of a prophet as one who is somber and angry—lashing out at unrighteousness. But they are thinking about Old Testament prophets, not those whom God is calling today.

You may ask, "Is a prophecy always fulfilled? Is it possible for a word from the Lord to not come to pass?"

If God says, "I will," then you can rest assured that is exactly what He plans to do. But there are conditions that He requires on our parts. They include faith, belief, and the act of receiving. If we choose not to follow through on the conditions, the promise might have to be passed on to our descendants.

I believe this is exactly how God works. Unfortunately, most people don't believe He means what He says. The Lord may deliver a word that says, "I'm going to heal you" or "I'm going to provide for you." Immediately that person may have an identity crisis and think, "I am not worthy. I'm still doing things that are wrong. This can't be God speaking to me!"

Here is what the Bible declares:

> *Therefore, as the Holy Spirit says: "Today, if you will hear His voice, do not harden your hearts as in the rebellion, in the day of trial in the wilderness, where your fathers tested Me, tried Me, and saw My works forty years"* (Hebrews 3:7-9).

God's Intentions Versus Our Actions

One of the biggest questions that people ask is: "Why did a prophecy not come to pass? Why did something that God Himself said not come to pass? What happened? Where did it go wrong?"

First of all, let me say this: God is never wrong! God is never wrong, and it is always man's fault—whether it is the prophet who made a mistake or whether it is the person who did something they were not supposed to do.

Think about this, God told Adam and Eve what His intentions were. The word to them was that they were going to subdue the earth and have dominion over all things. Well, rather than subduing, they were subdued. Whose fault was it that the word did not come to pass? Was it God's fault? Not at all. Did God know what was going to happen? Yes. Well, if God knew that, why did He say it?

God's intentions will not recognize any negative responses or actions. They will not even address the issue. There is a possibility that they exist, but when God speaks to you it is His intention to do it. Here is the final word. Even if His word is delayed by your failure, it does not mean that the word has failed. It will still be accomplished.

Some time ago, God spoke to me and said, "I want you to go to the United States of America and I am going to put you before presidents. I am going to put you before kings. You are going to prophesy to the nation. You are going to go to prisons. You are going to speak to the poor, to the pauper, and to the prince. And I am going to send you to the rich and poor, alike." God told me all this. Did it happen automatically and immediately? No! I had to leave my country and come to the United States. God could do absolutely nothing through me for this nation until I acted.

God demands the right response in order for His intention to become a manifested action. His intention is not always His action. God put us in time and space—gave us a will—and it is through the human will that God must act. God gave man the power to say no. God gave you the power to take an overdose and die or to just say no to drugs and live! You have the power over your life, to do well or to do evil to yourself and to your family.

So when God speaks, He is telling you what His intentions are as if you are going to follow the correct course in life in order to arrive at that place. He will speak to you His intentions as if He believed that you weren't going to do something stupid like become a druggie or jump off a building. God speaks to you as if you had no intentions of doing any wrong whatsoever. God believes that much in you. He never imagined the inconceivable.

It is important that you understand this, because do you know what I discovered? People who are unsaved often have more faith than the believer. The believer has a mind as well as a spirit, and here is the problem. Your mind is probably the most powerful thing that God has given you. *"Oh, I thought my spirit was!"* Your spirit affects your mind, but your mind is the most powerful thing. That is why He says that there must be a renewing of the mind, because the mind can get messed up. The spirit stays the same; but your mind can get messed up. You were designed in such a way that your spirit would control your thoughts and actions. Unfortunately, your mind is so powerful that it will often usurp the authority of your spirit. This is the battle that Paul describes in the Book of Romans.

Your mind is the battleground. Your mind is the place where the Spirit is pleading with you and saying, "Do not do this thing that you are considering within your mind. It will get you off course." God gives to all of us windows of opportunity. You and I have that little window of opportunity to do something wrong. But we also have that little window of opportunity to do something right. Whichever way we choose will eventually control our lives. We are partners with God, and if that partnership stays unbroken, then all of His promises will be fulfilled in our life.

If you want God's promise for tomorrow, here is what to do right now: *"Today...do not harden your hearts."* He leaves the choice to you.

To put it another way, if you harden your heart, today remains today and tomorrow will never come. God speaks *now* to prepare you for the future.

How to Enter Tomorrow

Why do people turn a deaf ear to God's voice? Because they do not know how the Lord operates. It was exactly the same with the children of Israel. The Lord said, "*They always go astray in their heart, and they have not known My ways*" (Heb. 3:10).

When God says, "I'm going to heal your disease," and the doctor says, "I'm giving you three months to live," most people say, "I don't see how God can make a way." They think God can't do it—and they turn away from God's voice. Why? Because they understand and can receive the natural voice far easier than the spiritual voice.

The message is clear. The generation of Israelites that hardened their hearts and refused the Lord's promise *stayed exactly where they were.* God said, "They shall not enter My rest" (Heb. 3:11).

When you don't receive the promise, time stands still, and you don't enter tomorrow. That is how God works. He waits to see the condition of your heart.

> *And to whom did He swear that they would not enter His rest, but to those who did not obey? So we see that they could not enter in because of unbelief* (Hebrews 3:18-19).

In the early days of Christ's ministry He "went about all Galilee, teaching in their synagogues, preaching the gospel of the kingdom, and healing all kinds of sickness and all kinds of disease among the people" (Matt. 4:23). But what happened when He went to Nazareth, His hometown? "He did not do many mighty works there because of their unbelief" (Matt. 13:58).

What is the "rest" the Lord spoke of in Hebrews 3? It is a rest from all our enemies. Scripture tells us that there will be a generation that experiences such a deliverance.

When the author of the Book of Hebrews wrote these words, no one had entered that rest. God promised it to the children of Israel, but they did not step out in faith and receive it. So the promise remains for you and for me.

> *Therefore, since a promise remains of entering His rest, let us fear lest any of you seem to have come short of it* (Hebrews 4:1).

The promise is not about heaven; it's about now. There is a generation that is to have dominion and subdue illness and iniquity.

What the Bible says next is at the heart of receiving a prophetic word.

> *For indeed the gospel was preached to us as well as to them; but the word which they heard did not profit them, not being mixed with faith in those who heard it* (Hebrews 4:2).

Yes, it is possible to receive a word from God and fail to benefit. Why? Because the message has not been combined with faith. It is only those who *believe* who can enter His rest.

> *Since therefore it remains that some must enter it, and those to whom it was first preached did not enter because of disobedience, again He designates a certain day, saying in David, "Today," after such a long time, as it has been said: "Today, if you will hear His voice, do not harden your hearts." For if Joshua had given them rest, then He would not afterward have spoken of another day* (Hebrews 4:6-8).

I believe God is still saying, "Today! Yield your heart to My word, and I will lead you into tomorrow." Again, the Bible says, "There remains therefore a rest for the people of God" (Heb. 4:9).

It is time to claim our inheritance and enter His rest.

ONLY A WORD

Many people are looking for God to come down from His throne and provide a miraculous deliverance. Instead, they need to be saying, "Lord, speak the word!"

A wonderful thing happened when Jesus went to Capernaum on the north shore of the Sea of Galilee. As the Lord entered the city, "a centurion came to Him, pleading with Him, saying, 'Lord, my servant is lying at home paralyzed, dreadfully tormented'" (Matt. 8:5-6).

Then Jesus made an offer that I cannot imagine anyone refusing. The Lord said, "I will come and heal him" (Matt. 8:7).

But the centurion—a Roman military officer in charge of hundreds of soldiers—turned to Christ and said, "Lord, I am not worthy that You should come under my roof. But only speak a word, and my servant will be healed" (Matt. 8:8). He didn't want a personal visit—just a word.

It was obvious that the centurion knew more about the authority of the Lord than many others of His day. The Jews, the covenant children of God, were void of such understanding. Even the disciples had difficulty comprehending what Christ meant when He said, "I am the way, the truth, and the life" (John 14:6), and "He who has seen Me has seen the Father" (John 14:9). They said among themselves, "What is this that He says to us?" (John 16:17).

The centurion understood the power of the spoken word. He said:

> *For I also am a man under authority, having soldiers under me. And I say to this one, "Go," and he goes; and to another, "Come," and he comes; and to my servant, "Do this," and he does it* (Matthew 8:9).

The Lord had never been approached in such a manner. Others came seeking His healing touch, but this man wanted only a word.

> *When Jesus heard it, He marveled, and said to those who followed, "Assuredly, I say to you, I have not found such great faith, not even in Israel!"…Then Jesus said to the centurion, "Go your way; and as you have believed, so let it be done for you." And his servant was healed that same hour* (Matthew 8:10,13).

The healing took place because the centurion had total faith in the voice of God. Jesus saw his heart and said, "As you have believed, so let it be done."

In my ministry I meet people every day who are praying for a visitation from the Lord. They want Him to come down from His throne and enter their homes. "Please, Lord," they cry, "come and touch me. Come and heal me!"

That is not how God operates today. Only once did God ever step out of eternity into time. He sent His Son to restore what was destroyed by satan in the Garden. Christ not only took on the physical form of man, but He took our sins to the cross. He died, rose again, and ascended to heaven.

Today it is not necessary for God to come to you. Instead, He has made it possible for you to have direct access to heaven. The Lord is saying, "Come and hear what I have to say. And when you hear My word, I'll pull back the curtain of time and show you the future."

When I hear the voice of the Lord, it is as though I am raised to higher ground, hearing the conversation of the Godhead in heavenly places. As the apostle Paul says, God has "raised us up together, and made us sit together in the heavenly places in Christ Jesus" (Eph. 2:6). Isaiah, too, heard the conversation of God when God brought him into His heavenly throne room.

Also I heard the voice of the Lord, saying: "Whom shall I send, And who will go for Us?" Then I said, "Here am I! Send me" (Isaiah 6:8).

I believe we can hear Jesus just as clearly as the apostle John did on the isle of Patmos. God confirmed that through John, saying:

Behold, I stand at the door and knock. If anyone hears My voice and opens the door, I will come in to him and dine with him, and he with Me (Revelation 3:20).

Perhaps you are beginning to know how I can have confidence when I look at someone and say, "God says you will not die. You will live!"

But when you have a prophetic word from God, you must realize that God has done His part. Now it is up to you. God waits to see if your heart agrees with what He has said.

WHOSE PROPHET IS GREATER?

At one of our crusades in South Africa we began to have a large number of Muslims attending the services. More than a thousand attended night after night because they heard that a prophet who represented Christ was in their city.

Many in the audience came because, as one man put it, "They wanted to make sure that their prophet is greater than the prophet of Christ."

That night the anointing of the Holy Spirit filled the auditorium. Suddenly I began to call out Muslims specifically—by name. It was one of the most unique meetings I have ever witnessed.

The Lord gave me the name Rajah. I called out the name, and Rajah stood up. I told him his home address and asked, "Is that where you live?" He said, "Yes."

"Rajah, come to the front," I said. "God wants to tell you something."

When he arrived at the platform, Rajah said, "But I am a Muslim."

"Well, I am a Christian. And God has given me a word for you. Jesus tells me that your father is dying of liver cancer and he's been given a few months left to live. But Jesus—not only the prophet, but the Son of God—says that you are to go and tell him that he is healed."

"Yes. What you say is true," said Rajah. "I will go and tell him."

Hundreds of Muslims came and were converted to Christ because of the voice of the Lord. There was such power in His word that on many nights they would literally run to the altar. God is not only alive, but He continues to speak to His people.

OPEN HEAVEN'S DOOR

When God spoke to Abraham, Isaac, Jacob, and other people in Old Testament times, He nearly always gave them a preview of what was about to happen next. It was to prove to them that the situation they were facing would be overcome.

Today, God also gives us a promise when He speaks to us. He says, "Behold, I stand at the door and knock. If anyone hears My voice and opens the door, I will come in to him and dine with him, and he with Me" (Rev. 3:20).

We usually think of these words in terms of the unsaved. But they also apply to those who are saved. (In fact, that verse was part of a message to the church of Laodicea.) The Lord says, "if" we hear His voice and open the door, He will be with us. Not "when," but "if." That same concept appears throughout Scripture.

> *If you will indeed obey My voice and keep My covenant, then you shall be a special treasure to Me* (Exodus 19:5).

> *And the Lord will make you the head and not the tail...if you heed the commandments of the Lord your God* (Deuteronomy 28:13).

> *If what you heard from the beginning abides in you, you also will abide in the Son and in the Father* (1 John 2:24).

The choice is yours: Will you listen to the sound of His voice or not? If you do choose to listen, then you must take action and spiritually "open" the door. Who opens it? *You* do!

Many people have been raised in an environment of mistrust. They have been wounded by other people so often that when God knocks at their door, they are afraid to open it. There is a vast difference, however, between the voice of God and the voice of man. Spend time with God. When you get to know the distinct sound of His voice, your heart will become tender to His call.

After these things I looked, and behold, a door standing open in heaven. And the first voice which I heard was like a trumpet speaking with me, saying, "Come up here, and I will show you things which must take place after this" (Revelation 4:1).

The voice did not say, "I am coming down to you." It said, "Come up here!"

Then, just as the Lord does for you and me, He gave John a promise. He said, "I will show you things which must take place after this." Tomorrow was about to be revealed.

When God told Abraham to offer Isaac as a sacrifice, God didn't come down from heaven. Instead, Abraham followed the Lord to the mountain. When Isaac was delivered, "Abraham called the name of the place, The-Lord-Will-Provide; as it is said to this day, 'In the Mount of the Lord it shall be provided'" (Gen. 22:14).

The Almighty did not descend from Mount Sinai to meet Moses. "The Lord called Moses to the top of the mountain, and Moses went up" (Exod. 19:20).

God has not changed. When He wants to speak to you, His voice calls you to where He is.

There is much more to life than a physical world and a human society. God longs to speak to your soul in a heavenly dimension. When you make the choice to open the door, the Lord begins to fulfill His incredible promises.

Chapter Five

"It's Not Over!"

The newspaper reporter asked, "Mr. Clement, what is a white man from South Africa going to tell the people of our country?"

I was in Perth, a city of over one million people in Western Australia.

Immediately I knew what the journalist meant. I said, "I am not here to represent South Africa. And I certainly won't be talking about apartheid or politics."

I felt like telling him what I had suffered because of standing with black people during my lifetime. But I was not there to vindicate myself or promote any causes.

"Then why did you come?" he asked.

"I am here to represent the Kingdom of God. I have come to reach the unreachable and touch the untouchable."

The next day those words were on the front page of the newspaper—so were my picture and a story about the evangelistic crusade moving to a large auditorium.

About two weeks earlier I had come to Perth at the invitation of a local pastor. Just a handful of people attended the first service. But they were hungry for a word from God.

The Lord began to move in such an unusual way that the people were coming from everywhere. There was such a wonderful outpouring of God's Spirit that within a few nights the building was jammed to capacity.

Several ministers in the area saw what God was doing and came to visit me. They said, "We believe we should turn this into a citywide campaign. Will you stay in Perth if we can arrange it?"

"Yes," I told them. "God is about to do something supernatural."

The Entertainment Center in Perth seats about 6,000, and they arranged to move the meetings there. "We can cordon it off to seat 4,000," one of the preachers said. "The last evangelistic crusade we had drew about 2,200."

"I've got shocking news for you," I told them. "If God sends His word, the people will come. Open it up! We'll fill that place."

SOMEONE FAMOUS?

For two weeks—ever since I arrived in Perth—I had felt such a burden for Western Australia that I had entered a time of total fasting and prayer. I had not touched a scrap of food and had drunk only water. "Lord," I prayed, "send Your word. Send Your word."

The day we moved to the Entertainment Center the front page news story appeared. It said, "I have come to reach the unreachable and touch the untouchable."

Thousands and thousands of people poured into the arena. The moment I walked onto the platform I could feel a special surge of God's power. It was like electricity. Even though I was weak from fasting, I felt ten feet tall.

While the large choir was singing, I prayed, "Lord, do something unusual tonight. We need to reach this city for You."

I was hoping that God would give me a prophetic word for some well-known person in the audience. "Bring someone who is famous into the Kingdom," I prayed. "It will be such an example." I thought that perhaps a senator, an actor, a sports celebrity, or a television reporter would be perfect. I wanted to see something so profound that people would go away saying, "Can you believe what happened tonight?"

I should have known that God doesn't speak because of my desires, but because of His will.

As the meeting proceeded, the choir sang "Amazing Grace," and I preached for about 30 minutes under a strong anointing. The power of the Lord so filled that auditorium that people were being saved, healed, and baptized in the Spirit. But I continued to pray, "Lord, I know that You have a prophetic word for someone special here tonight. Show me the man or woman You are going to speak to."

As I was looking for direction from the Lord, I noticed a group of well-dressed people seated together, and I thought, *Surely it is one of them. Lord, do You have a special word I can give?* But nothing came.

Then I felt an urging in my spirit that said, "Look at the back of the auditorium. Do you see that seat at the end of the aisle in the last row? That's where I want you to go!"

I thought, *Have I heard correctly? Who would be so important that they would be sitting in the last row?*

As I walked through the huge auditorium, I looked to my left and to my right for someone to whom the Lord would direct me to speak. But the only thing He said was, "I won't tell you anything until you go to the last seat in the last row."

People turned their heads and watched me intently as I continued to walk. They wondered whom I was going to call out. Whom was I going to prophesy over?

When I reached the back wall of the building, I saw the seat God had pointed out to me. Then, when I saw the person seated there, I thought, *This is impossible. Why would God have me speak to this person?*

In front of me was a disheveled teenager whose shirt was tattered and torn. I tried to disregard the odor of his body as I looked at his eyes. They were vacant and wounded with pain.

For a second I was frozen. Then God said to me, "Remember yourself! That's you!"

I suddenly saw myself as a wasted young man, high on heroin, stabbed and bleeding to death on a street in Port Elizabeth. And I remembered how someone came to my rescue and led me to the Savior. Those years of drugs, rock, and rebellion had disappeared when the Lord penetrated my heart.

Now it was my turn to rescue someone else.

I called the young man by his name, and he recoiled like a frightened child. "Come with me," I said as I led him down the long aisle to the platform.

As we stood in front of that audience, I put my arms around him and said, "God says for me to tell you: 'This day I have become your Father.'"

The young man began to cry, embraced me, and asked for prayer.

BULLETS IN THE BARREL

I learned later that just three days before the meeting a dramatic story had been unfolding in the life of this 16-year-old boy. He had been in his hometown of Sydney, the largest city in Australia. Sydney was more than 2,000 miles away from Perth. His father was an alcoholic and a hopeless drug addict. His mother had died because of a horrible beating—and his father had been accused of doing it.

The son, who was also on drugs, had come home one day and been severely beaten by his father. He had been literally kicked out of the door. He had broken bones, and he was bleeding. His father yelled, "I never want to see you again. Never! Never!" Then he said, "Today I disown you! I am not your father anymore!"

"It's Not Over!"

The young man took some of the last drugs he had, stumbled to the home of a friend, and borrowed a gun. He had put some bullets in it and said to himself, *It's over!* He was ready to take his own life. But instead, for no reason at all, he walked to the highway and began to hitchhike across Australia.

Three days later, still alone, he found himself sitting on the curb of a street in downtown Perth. He was still contemplating suicide.

Perth is a windy city, and suddenly a sheet of newspaper blew near him. He grabbed it. He was going to roll a "joint" and have a smoke. As he was about to tear the paper, he saw the word *unreachable* on the page. Next to it was my picture. The word seemed to jump right off the paper. *Unreachable*, he thought. *That's me!*

The scruffy teen said to himself, *I need to get to this man if it's the last thing I do. Perhaps he has something to tell me.*

He looked back at the newspaper. The article said that I was going to be at the Entertainment Center. He glanced up and immediately saw the name of the building across the street: Entertainment Center. The doors were just opening for the first meeting.

He walked in and took a seat on the last row. As he waited for the service to begin, he thought, *I don't know if God knows me or cares about me. I don't know if Jesus exists, but I hope that God will do something for me.*

Now, standing on the platform, he was welcomed into the family of God.

The Christians in that city received him as one of their own. He was filled with the Spirit and began reaching out to young people on the streets of Australia.

God knew who was the most important person in that service. We can always trust the sound of His voice.

Whom Does He Call?

Those who despised Christ and His followers scoffed whenever He talked with those who were despised. Do you remember what the Pharisees said when Jesus began speaking to a prostitute?

A woman in the city who was a sinner, when she knew that Jesus sat at the table in the Pharisee's house, brought an alabaster flask of fragrant oil, and stood at His feet behind Him weeping; and she began to wash His feet with her tears, and wiped them with the hair of her head; and she kissed His feet and anointed them with the fragrant oil. Now when the Pharisee who had invited Him saw this, he spoke to himself, saying, "This Man, if He were a prophet, would know who and what manner of woman this is who is touching Him, for she is a sinner" (Luke 7:37-39).

They did not understand that the Lord responds to faith, regardless of who the person might be. Jesus said, "I did not come to call the righteous, but sinners, to repentance" (Matt. 9:13). What did Christ tell the critical Pharisee?

"Therefore I say to you, her sins, which are many, are forgiven, for she loved much. But to whom little is forgiven, the same loves little." Then He said to her, "Your sins are forgiven" (Luke 7:47-48).

A gentleman in Florida recently asked me, "Does a person have to be righteous to receive the voice of the Lord?"

"Of course not," I replied. "Even though prophecy is primarily for the Church, God has always used His voice to redeem humanity and to reveal His plans."

Jacob, the son of Isaac, was not exactly an honorable man. He was a liar and a deceiver. He tricked his brother, Esau, out of his birthright for some bread and some lentil stew (see Gen. 25:29-34). And Jacob even received his father's blessing by disguising himself as Esau (see Gen. 27:1-41).

Nevertheless, God spoke to Jacob through a vision while he was sleeping on the ground with a stone for a pillow.

Then he dreamed, and behold, a ladder was set up on the earth, and its top reached to heaven; and there the angels of God were ascending and descending on it. And behold, the Lord stood above it and said: "I am the Lord God of Abraham your father and the God of Isaac; the land on which you lie I will give to you and your descendants" (Genesis 28:12-13).

The Lord gave Jacob this promise:

Your descendants shall be as the dust of the earth; you shall spread abroad to the west and the east, to the north and the south; and in you and in your seed all the families of the earth shall be blessed. Behold, I am with you and will keep you wherever you go; and will bring you back to this land; for I will not leave you until I have done what I have spoken to you (Genesis 28:14-15).

The man who lied and deceived was even given a brand-new name. God said, "Your name shall not be called Jacob anymore, but Israel shall be your name" (Gen. 35:10). And he became the father of the 12 tribes of Israel. God speaks to your destiny and your future, not your past. God spoke to the "Israel" in Jacob, and therefore the "Israel" was released out of Jacob.

THOUGHTS FROM ABOVE

How does God accomplish His prophetic word? It begins with just a thought. God thinks about something. And we become in harmony with God—"tuned in" to His thoughts. We begin to understand what He wants us to know. " 'For I know the thoughts that I think toward you,' says the Lord, 'thoughts of peace and not of evil, to give you a future and a hope'" (Jer. 29:11).

There was a person in the Bible who had a special understanding of the thoughts of the Lord. His name was David. The confidence David established in his relationship with the Lord was evident. His prayer to the Lord was "Keep me as the apple of Your eye" (Ps. 17:8).

It was David who said, "How precious also are Your thoughts to me, O God! How great is the sum of them! If I should count them, they would be more in number than the sand" (Ps. 139:17-18).

Have you ever wondered what God is thinking about you?

It starts as a thought, then it becomes a word.

God was speaking of His everlasting covenant to David when He said, "For My thoughts are not your thoughts, nor are your ways My ways" (Isa. 55:8). This was not a statement of unbelief, but a plea from the heart of God. The Lord was saying, "I want My thoughts to become your thoughts. I want My ways to become your ways."

God says, "For as the heavens are higher than the earth, so are My ways higher than your ways, and My thoughts than your thoughts" (Isa. 55:9). He not only wants to lift the level of our listening, but also desires that we know His mind.

If you could have just a glimpse of what God thinks about you, you would become a new person. His esteem for you is greater than you have for yourself.

Most people think God changes His mind about them because of their mistakes or failures. That may be how your friends and neighbors respond, but not God. He created you in His image and sees the potential of your life.

Society teaches us to believe "three strikes, and you're out." But life is not a ball game with a rigid set of rules. And our alliance with God is not a legal contract, but a working relationship—a love covenant between you and your Creator.

What happens when a small child makes a mistake? Is the child banished from the family? No. And God treats us the same way.

It is vital that we seek to know God's thoughts because they are the source of what He says. His mind becomes His voice. He declares:

> *For as the rain comes down, and the snow from heaven, and do not return there, but water the earth, and make it bring forth and bud, that it may give seed to the sower, and bread to the eater, so shall My word be that goes forth from My mouth, it shall not return to Me void, but it shall accomplish what I please, and it shall prosper in the thing for which I sent it* (Isaiah 55:10-11).

God's words are *committed* words. When the Lord sends a word to you that says, for example, "Your child will come out of drugs," that is a commitment from the Lord on which He will never turn His back.

We need always to remember that the moment God says something to you, it is already a fact. And He gives you His pledge to uphold His part of the bargain.

God has made a commitment, but what about you? What is your part? If you believe that God must accomplish His prophetic word, you are mistaken. When the Lord begins to speak, it is your choice to accept it, believe it, and act upon it. When God speaks, a door is opened for us. But we have to step through if we are to see the promise become a reality.

"We Are Waiting!"

Before Christ returned to heaven, He made a promise that God's voice would continue to speak to you and me. "And I will pray the Father, and He will give you another Helper, that He may abide with you forever—the Spirit of truth" (John 14:16-17).

Then Jesus said that when the Holy Spirit comes, "He will guide you into all truth; for He will not speak on His own authority, but whatever He hears He will speak; and He will tell you things to come" (John 16:13).

The prophetic word is part of the trinity. From the moment of creation, the voice of God has revealed the future. When Christ was sent to earth, He also spoke about tomorrow. Now the Holy Spirit was about to descend. He would also speak of "things to come."

Jesus "commanded them not to depart from Jerusalem, but to wait for the Promise of the Father, 'which,' He said, 'you have heard from Me; for John truly baptized with water, but you shall be baptized with the Holy Spirit not many days from now'" (Acts 1:4-5).

When Christ had returned to Heaven, 120 believers gathered in the upper room. They began waiting on God. I can imagine them praying, "Father, we know that Jesus was the Word, but You promised us something more. Lord, You said something about a Comforter. You said something about One who would be by our side. We are waiting! We are waiting!"

Then it happened!

Suddenly there came a sound from heaven, as of a rushing mighty wind, and it filled the whole house where they were sitting. Then there appeared to them divided tongues, as of fire, and one sat upon each of them. And they were all filled with the Holy Spirit, and began to speak with other tongues, as the Spirit gave them utterance (Acts 2:2-4).

There was not only a sound, but there was also a *breath.* And they became the voice of God. Their sound was then translated into languages so that all could hear the message of God.

A TRIPLE RESTORATION

As I learned at that meeting in Western Australia, we don't always understand why God speaks as He does. But when the promise is ultimately revealed, we can see God's hand at work.

That was certainly true in the life of Simon Peter. Discovering how God dealt with him through prophecy is like finding the answer to how God speaks—and *why* He speaks.

So many people are like Peter. They have failed God miserably and feel ashamed to face Him. They hide themselves away and say, "Lord, I know I am never going to be used again because I have sinned." But if they will listen, God has a word of restoration.

Without question, Peter committed one of the most serious spiritual crimes possible. He denied the Lord Jesus Christ—not once, but three times.

Just before the crucifixion, while the high priest was questioning Jesus, Peter was waiting outside the courtyard.

> *Then the servant girl who kept the door said to Peter, "You are not also one of this Man's disciples, are you?" He said, "I am not"* (John 18:17).

A few minutes later, while he was warming himself by a fire, someone else asked Peter, "You are not also one of His disciples, are you?" He denied it and said, "I am not!" (John 18:25).

Then one of the servants of the high priest, a relative of him whose ear Peter cut off, said, "Did I not see you in the garden with Him?"

Peter then denied knowing Jesus again (see John 18:26-27).

The story does not end with Peter's being rejected by the Almighty. Far from it. After the resurrection of Jesus, it is thrilling to see how God changes Peter's life. He had denied the Lord three times, but Christ offered him restoration three times.

Jesus appeared to His disciples at the shore of the Sea of Tiberias while they were fishing. When they came to the shore and all had breakfast together, Jesus said to Simon Peter:

> *"Simon, son of Jonah, do you love me more than these?"*
> *He said to Him, "Yes, Lord; You know that I love You."*

He said to him, "Feed My lambs."
He said to him again a second time, "Simon, son of Jonah,
do you love Me?"
He said to Him, "Yes, Lord; You know that I love You."
He said to him, "Tend My sheep."
He said to him the third time, "Simon, son of Jonah, do you
love Me?" Peter was grieved because He said to him the third
time, "Do you love Me?"
And he said to Him, "Lord, You know all things; You know
that I love You."
Jesus said to him, "Feed My sheep" (John 21:15-17).

Before God revealed His plan for Peter's future, He dealt with the matter of restoration.

It is tragic that when people sin, they believe they can never be restored. But if you are *willing* to be reconciled to Christ, He is waiting to receive you.

A PROPHECY FROM JESUS TO PETER

After Simon Peter experienced God's forgiveness and was once again secure in Christ, God gave him a prophetic word. It was an unusual message.

Most assuredly, I say to you, when you were younger, you
girded yourself and walked where you wished; but when you
are old, you will stretch out your hands, and another will gird
you and carry you where you do not wish (John 21:18).

Those were words that Peter did not want to hear. He probably wondered what they meant. Was Christ talking about how he was going to die?

The first time I read those words I thought, *Is that really a significant prophecy? Where is the hope? Where is the promise?*

Peter may have interpreted the words to mean, "When I die, someone is going to dress me and carry me to the grave."

But Jesus was telling him something about tomorrow that was more positive and powerful than Peter could comprehend, as we will see.

So often we want to hear powerful words from God. I'm sure Peter would have liked Jesus to prophesy, "One day you are going to preach in Jerusalem, and 3,000 will be saved! You are going to pray for a crippled man at the temple gate, and he will be healed! You are going to lay your hands on people, and they will receive the Holy Spirit!"

What we must realize, however, is that *any* utterance that comes from the mouth of God has the power to release great miracles in our lives.

A Voice in Prison

When Christ ascended to heaven, Peter began his ministry. The anointing he received in the upper room resulted in an unparalleled spread of the gospel. There were signs, wonders, and miracles at every turn.

Peter became a new man. When he opened his mouth to speak, he had a new power. Thousands were added to the Kingdom of God.

From that day until now satan has been trying to stop that resurrection power. One of his initial attempts was to have Peter executed.

> *Now about that time Herod the king stretched out his hand to harass some from the church. Then he killed James the brother of John with the sword. And because he saw that it pleased the Jews, he proceeded further to seize Peter also. Now it was during the Days of Unleavened Bread. So when he had arrested him, he put him in prison, and delivered him to four squads of soldiers to keep him, intending to bring him before the people after Passover* (Acts 12:1-4).

It is difficult to imagine what Peter was thinking when he knew James was beheaded by the soldiers. Would he be next?

What would be the result of the mock trial that soon would take place? I'm sure he thought about the foreboding words of Herod: "I'm going to kill you after the Passover."

But while Peter was kept in prison, "constant prayer was offered to God for him by the church" (Acts 12:5).

The night before Herod was to bring him to trial, "Peter was sleeping, bound with two chains between two soldiers; and the guards before the door were keeping the prison" (Acts 12:6).

How could Peter sleep in the face of such adversity? I believe that Peter went to prison filled with fear. But he began to pray, "God, reveal Your will to me. Please rescue me! Do You have a word I can cling to?"

While he was praying Peter might have said, "Lord, what did You tell me at the shore of the sea?" And he heard a still, small voice echo four words of Jesus: "When you are old!"

Perhaps he recalled the prophecy of Jesus and knew there would be no execution. What had Jesus told him? "When you are old, you will stretch out your hands, and another will gird you and carry you where you do not wish" (John 21:18).

I believe Peter must have looked at himself and said, "I'm not an old man! I am still young! This is not my time to die!"

The words of Christ were not of death, but of hope and expectation. Suddenly the words of Christ flooded his spirit, and he entered God's peace. He fell asleep and waited for the deliverance of the Lord.

> *Now behold, an angel of the Lord stood by him, and a light shone in the prison; and he struck Peter on the side and raised him up, saying, "Arise quickly!" And his chains fell off his hands* (Acts 12:7).

Think of it! While Peter was waiting for his execution, he was sleeping so soundly that, even with a bright light shining, the angel had to strike him to wake him up. He was totally resting in the promise.

The words that were spoken next were an amazing fulfillment of Christ's prophecy.

Then the angel said to him, "Gird yourself and tie on your sandals"; and so he did. And he said to him, "Put on your garment and follow me" (Acts 12:8).

Why did the angel say "gird yourself"? Because Jesus had told Peter, "When you are old...another will gird you."

Why did the angel say "tie on your sandals" and "follow me"? Because Jesus told Peter that when he was old he wouldn't be able to walk by himself. The Lord said, "Another will...carry you."

This was not Peter's time to die! He was going to live. No one else was going to dress him. He was still young and alive.

And when Peter had come to himself, he said, "Now I know for certain that the Lord has sent His angel, and has delivered me from the hand of Herod and from all the expectation of the Jewish people" (Acts 12:11).

Never take lightly the voice of God. He gives you His word to use as a weapon against the powers of darkness that come against you. In the hour of your greatest battle you can cling to His promise and rest with great joy and confidence.

The time may come when you are in a prison of physical illness, bound by financial needs, or, like the young man in Australia, abandoned and trapped by the pressures of life. But that is when you will hear the voice of God say, "It's not over! I have a great work for you to accomplish!"

Chapter Six

The Great Transformation

When God rescued me from a self-destructive spiral of drugs and rebellion that left me dying in a gutter, I wanted to give Him my best. Everything about God's Word, Christian living, and the church was new. All I could pray was, "Lord, all that I have is Yours. You have given me musical talent that I want to use for Your glory."

I waited and waited for God to reply. I was hoping that He would say, "I will greatly multiply your gift. Your songs will be used mightily to build the Kingdom."

But instead the Lord said, "Kim, I am calling you to a prophetic ministry."

A prophet? I wondered. *Why would the Lord call me to be a prophet?*

But God had spoken. What I later learned was that when God speaks, He creates something from nothing—something that was not there before. Why does He operate in such a manner? I believe it is so we cannot take the glory or credit for His manifestation. It is important that the world be compelled to say, "That is God, not man."

Three important things happen when God speaks:

- He creates.

- He forms.
- He transforms.

And something more. God vindicates His transformation by giving us His oil of anointing.

There is nothing to compare with God's "creative word." He does not speak something into your life that you already have; He creates something that you don't already possess. The way God causes that to happen, however, is quite unusual. Many people believe that God always creates a finished product immediately. But one meaning for the word *create* in the Bible is to "fashion something"—to "prepare" it for habitation.

I like to think of God's prophetic words as an outer shell that He allows to be filled and completed. For example, being born again and becoming a new creation in Christ are only the beginning of what we will become. God first creates something, and then He inhabits it.

Every time God speaks to you—whether it is through an individual or during a time of meditation and prayer—His creation is at work. It's like a burst of energy that explodes within your spirit. Suddenly, you possess something you did not have before. And that is just the start.

SQUEEZING AND FASHIONING

Immediately after God speaks something into creation, He takes the second step: He *forms.* First God *said,* "Let Us make man" (Gen. 1:26). He "created man in His own image" (Gen. 1:27). How did God do it? By forming him.

And the Lord God formed man of the dust of the ground, and breathed into his nostrils the breath of life; and man became a living being (Genesis 2:7).

Most people are in a big hurry. "Lord, I need to hear from You right now," they pray. But when God speaks, we don't always see the final product instantly. After He creates us, He begins the process of squeezing each contour and fashioning each profile. And all the time He is watching our response.

I once was asked, "If God created every person, why do some turn out to be saints and others sinners? Why are some parents loving and kind, while others are cruel and abusive?"

Why do some people become liars, murderers, and thieves? They reach that state by rebelling against God's attempts to form them. As free moral agents, they choose the path they travel.

Between creation and formation the Lord gives us the option to either accept or reject His redemptive plan. Your refusal of salvation allows satan to take your carnal clay and fashion it into something evil.

When the Bible says that we are "to be conformed to the image of His Son" (Rom. 8:29), it means that we are to be fashioned or shaped into the Lord's likeness.

We serve an imaginative and creative God. When He speaks, He creates something totally distinctive and fresh. It is almost impossible to comprehend that there are more than five billion people on earth, yet no two people have identical fingerprints or DNA.

In my travels I am constantly amazed by the people I meet. Every personality is distinct—each with its own disposition, nature, and temperament. And in all these people is a constant flow of fresh creativity. How exciting it is that each person has a spiritual personality that is being formed into the image of Christ.

When God calls people to His service, He gives them a unique ministry. But some people find that difficult to understand. Many young evangelists have stood before mirrors and tried to look and sound like Billy Graham or Oral Roberts. They wanted to imitate every vocal inflection and every gesture. But God has not called you to be someone else. He has called you to be you!

*But now, thus says the Lord, **who created you**, O Jacob, And He who **formed you**, O Israel: "Fear not, for I have redeemed you; I have called you by your name; you are mine"* (Isaiah 43:1, emphasis added).

We all have our own personalities and our own names. But into whose image does God want to shape us? *His* image.

Paul, writing to the church at Galatia, described spiritual formation as being like a woman giving birth to a child. It is accomplished by travail, anguish, and suffering. But that is nothing compared with what is brought into the world through the pain—the baby!

It is good to be zealous in a good thing always, and not only when I am present with you. My little children, for whom I labor in birth again until Christ is formed in you... (Galatians 4:18-19).

Always remember—we first become a new creation, then we are formed.

THE BREATH OF LIFE

What happens next is even more inspiring. After God creates us and forms us, He *transforms* us.

Do you remember what happened after God formed man? He "breathed into his nostrils the breath of life" (Gen. 2:7) and transformed Adam into a living being.

Today that important work is accomplished through the Holy Spirit. The breath of the Lord also imparts the Spirit. Just after the resurrection, Jesus gathered His disciples together and said:

"Peace to you! As the Father has sent Me, I also send you." And when He had said this, He breathed on them, and said to them, "Receive the Holy Spirit" (John 20:21-22).

As millions of people can testify, that same power is still available.

116

It is the transforming power of the Spirit that makes it possible for us to be in the presence of the Lord. On the Mount of Transfiguration, Christ was changed from one state of existence to another. Scripture records that "the appearance of His face was altered, and His robe became white and glistening" (Luke 9:29).

Centuries before, God's presence was so mighty on Moses that "the children of Israel could not look steadily at the face of Moses because of the glory of his countenance" (2 Cor. 3:7).

When he came down from Mount Sinai to deliver the Covenant, "the skin of Moses' face shone, then Moses would put the veil on his face" (Exod. 34:35).

But now the covenant is "written not with ink but by the Spirit of the living God, not on tablets of stone but on tablets of flesh, that is, of the heart" (2 Cor. 3:3). Because of the change that happens inside, we become transformed so that we are able to look directly into the face of the Lord. It is possible because "when one turns to the Lord, the veil is taken away" (2 Cor. 3:16).

Through the power of the Spirit "we all, with unveiled face, beholding as in a mirror the glory of the Lord, are being transformed into the same image from glory to glory, just as by the Spirit of the Lord" (2 Cor. 3:18).

You may ask, "Do I have to wait until I get to Heaven to be transformed?"

No. It happens now. "Therefore, if anyone is in Christ, he is a new creation; old things have passed away; behold, all things have become new" (2 Cor. 5:17).

In our natural state we cannot become the voice of God to the world. We might have the best education and speak eloquently, but our effort will be meaningless. It is only when the Spirit changes us that we can minister healing and deliverance in the name of the Lord. That's what gives us authority over satan and the ability to touch the untouchable.

The Lord forms us by dealing with our spirits and our souls. But when we are transformed, it allows the formation that has taken place to be expressed outwardly. It is something that comes from the inside out.

When the glory of God descended on Christ, the outward manifestation of what had taken place inside was evident in His face being altered and His robe glistening white. When did that glory descend upon Jesus? The glory came from the voice as Peter testifies in his Epistle: "For He received from God the Father honour and glory, when there came such a voice to Him from the excellent glory, This is My beloved Son, in whom I am well pleased" (2 Pet. 1:17 KJV). It is the voice of God that brings the glory of God.

A METAMORPHOSIS

More than once I have seen sincere people attempt to operate in the realm of the Spirit without first being transformed. They have read enough Scripture to know what is available, but they have never allowed the Lord to "breathe" on them. You will be glorified and elevated when the voice of God comes to you. It is the sound of His voice that empowers us for change.

I beseech you therefore, brethren, by the mercies of God, that you present your bodies a living sacrifice, holy, acceptable to God, which is your reasonable service. And do not be conformed to this world, but be transformed by the renewing of your mind, that you may prove [show forth, express] *what is that good and acceptable and perfect will of God* (Romans 12:1-2).

There is a big difference between being conformed and being transformed. In the world of science, a total transformation is called a metamorphosis. That is what happens when a fuzzy caterpillar sheds its skin and becomes a butterfly, or when a tadpole comes out of the water and turns into a frog.

Throughout the New Testament we are warned against being formed into the mold of this world. Paul tells us that the transformation that should take place includes a new source of knowledge.

Now we have received, not the spirit of the world, but the Spirit who is from God, that we might know the things that have been freely given to us by God (1 Corinthians 2:12).

Who is our teacher?

These things we also speak, not in words which man's wisdom teaches but which the Holy Spirit teaches, comparing spiritual things with spiritual. But the natural man does not receive the things of the Spirit of God, for they are foolishness to him, nor can he know them, because they are spiritually discerned. But he who is spiritual judges all things, yet he himself is rightly judged by no one (1 Corinthians 2:13-15).

Every day we need to claim God's promise that the Spirit will illuminate our thought lives. We need to pray that knowledge of the Word will transform us—that there will be an outward expression of what is taking place within.

CHAPTER SEVEN

DEFILEMENT
BY DIVINATION

Throughout history man has longed to become divine.

In ancient Rome, Caesar Augustus, Nero, and other emperors declared themselves to be divine, and people likened them unto gods. The same was true of rulers in ancient Greece.

For centuries the monarchs of England, France, and Germany said that their power derived from "the divine right of kings"—that this right to rule came directly from God. Accordingly, it was up to the Almighty, not the subjects, to punish a wicked king.

The desire to be superhuman is also seen in athletics. World-class competitors will do almost anything in their quest for greatness. They crave to be heralded as the strongest or swiftest.

Canadian track star Ben Johnson wanted to become the "world's fastest man" at the Seoul Olympics in 1988. He was so obsessed by his goal that he resorted to taking drugs to enhance his speed. As a result, his dreams were dashed, and he was stripped of his titles.

What the world seeks through earthly means can be ours through being children of the living God. We have been given the ability to become partakers of the divine. He allows us to receive the essence of His godliness, personality, and character.

As I will describe in the rest of this chapter, God has chosen to share with us a divine nature, divine power, and a divine inheritance.

A New Nature

Peter, who was an eyewitness to the transfiguration of Christ, explains how it is possible for us to participate in the very nature of God. He was not writing to the unbeliever, but to "those who have obtained like precious faith with us by the righteousness of our God and Savior Jesus Christ" (2 Pet. 1:1).

Peter said:

> *His divine power has given to us all things that pertain to life and godliness, through the knowledge of Him who called us by glory and virtue, by which have been given to us exceedingly great and precious promises, that through these you may be **partakers of the divine nature**, having escaped the corruption that is in the world through lust* (2 Peter 1:3-4, emphasis added).

The voice of God is a voice of promise, and this is one of God's greatest commitments: We are to become "partakers of the divine."

Becoming a partaker means that we share in something but do not totally possess it. In other words, we are only partaking in that substance called divinity. We participate in His purposes by being a divine expression of His nature here on this earth. Because of this unique union, God can minister to us, speak through us, and allow us to become His representatives.

In your daily routine of driving to work, dealing with business matters, or raising a family, you may say, "I certainly don't feel divine."

Well, you are not! You are only a *partaker* of the divine. But God can express His heavenly nature through you whenever He pleases—on a bus, in a car, or at home. Suddenly He comes upon you, and the divine is expressed as you utter the will of God in a specific situation.

We are not puppets walking through the earth without purpose. His will is accomplished through our affinity with Him. The attributes, the properties, and the nature of God are allowed to flow through us. It is part of our heritage as children of God.

Because of the work of Christ on the cross, we have a divine nature.

SORCERY IN SAMARIA

When the world sees the power of God operating in the lives of believers, it is only natural for them to covet the same blessing. They become so envious that they attempt to imitate the divine. That is what happened in Samaria.

A genuine revival was taking place in the city through the ministry of Philip.

The multitudes with one accord heeded the things spoken by Philip, hearing and seeing the miracles which he did. For unclean spirits, crying with a loud voice, came out of many who were possessed; and many who were paralyzed and lame were healed (Acts 8:6-7).

But another man in the city had enjoyed the respect of the people before Philip came.

There was a certain man called Simon, who previously practiced sorcery in the city and astonished the people of Samaria, claiming that he was someone great, to whom they all gave heed, from the least to the greatest, saying, "This man is the great power of God." And they heeded him because he had astonished them with his sorceries for a long time (Acts 8:9-11).

Because Simon astounded them with his evil supernatural powers, they actually heralded him as being "the great power of God."

We need to be cautious of people—even inside the Church—who astonish us with their exploits. Astonishment is not enough. We need to observe their lives and determine that they have truly been transformed. We must see conviction, repentance, love, and unity.

When people have never experienced the power of the Lord, they will call almost anything divine. The disciples themselves knew how it felt to have people elevate them to a position far higher than the Lord intended (see Acts 14:8-18; 28:1-6).

For years the people had treated Simon as someone divine. The Bible says they "heeded" his words. Then the gospel was preached in Samaria with authority, anointing, and power. Scripture records that "when they believed Philip as he preached the things concerning the kingdom of God and the name of Jesus Christ, both men and women were baptized" (Acts 8:12).

What a difference the name of Jesus makes! People were coming to Christ in great numbers. But what about Simon? How did he respond?

Then Simon himself also believed; and when he was baptized he continued with Philip, and was amazed, seeing the miracles and signs which were done (Acts 8:13).

The sorcerer was saved! He became a friend to Philip and observed firsthand the healing and deliverance that was taking place. That's why he was on hand when the believers first received the Holy Spirit.

Now when the apostles who were at Jerusalem heard that Samaria had received the word of God, they sent Peter and John to them, who, when they had come down, prayed for them that they might receive the Holy Spirit. For as yet He had

fallen upon none of them. They had only been baptized in the
name of the Lord Jesus. Then they laid hands on them, and
they received the Holy Spirit (Acts 8:14-17).

For the first time since Christ ascended to heaven, God's
glory was being transferred from one person to another. Peter
and John were sent by the church at Jerusalem to see what was
happening in Samaria. They began laying hands on people to
receive the Spirit.

In the Old Testament, laying on of hands was used to con-
fer blessing (see Gen. 48:13-20), to transfer guilt from the sinner
to the sacrifice (see Lev. 1:4), and to commission someone for a
God-ordained responsibility. Moses brought Joshua before the
priest, "And he laid his hands on him and inaugurated him, just
as the Lord commanded" (Num. 27:23).

When Christ came to the earth, He continued the practice.
Jesus brought healing to the leper as He "stretched out His
hand and touched him, and said to him, 'I am willing; be
cleansed'" (Mark 1:41). He gathered children around Him,
"laid His hands on them, and blessed them" (Mark 10:16).

What Peter and John were imparting was more than a blessing. They were transferring the very power of God through the
Holy Spirit. It was a power that Simon had never seen before,
and immediately he wanted that same ability. But he was totally
ignorant regarding how God chose to deliver the Spirit. He
thought the gift could be purchased.

When Simon saw that through the laying on of the apostles'
hands the Holy Spirit was given, he offered them money, say-
ing, "Give me this power also, that anyone on whom I lay
hands may receive the Holy Spirit" (Acts 8:18-19).

Simon had been saved and baptized but had much to learn
about spiritual gifts. He did not understand that the power of
God is not for sale. He probably thought that his sorcery
brought him great esteem, fame, and fortune. If he gave these

men a substantial sum of money, perhaps they would give this new power to him.

The price Peter and John paid for the anointing, however, was much different. The authority that rested on them came through prayer, fasting, suffering, and travail—along with love, joy, and worship.

But like so many people who want to display the divine, Simon wanted easy access and instant results. He wanted to take control of the power of God and offered payment for the privilege.

Many might be tempted by material gain. But not Peter. He said to Simon, "Your money perish with you, because you thought that the gift of God could be purchased with money!" (Acts 8:20).

Simon probably had heard about what had happened to Ananias and Sapphira. They perished when Peter exposed them for lying to the Holy Spirit about an offering they had given to the apostles (see Acts 5:11).

Now Peter was giving a similar warning to Simon. Because the new convert thought he could purchase the power of the Spirit, Peter told him, "Your money perish with you." Then he added, "You have neither part nor portion in this matter, for your heart is not right in the sight of God. Repent therefore of this your wickedness, and pray God if perhaps the thought of your heart may be forgiven you" (Acts 8:21-22).

Peter did not promise forgiveness. He asked Simon to repent and to pray that the Lord "perhaps" might pardon his transgression. The disciple told him, "I see that you are poisoned by bitterness and bound by iniquity" (Acts 8:23).

Then Simon answered and said, "Pray to the Lord for me, that none of the things which you have spoken may come upon me" (Acts 8:24).

Just because a person believes on Christ does not automatically qualify him to receive everything that is divine. The transference that takes place by the laying on of hands is sacred. It must never be given to someone who is not right before God.

PSYCHICS

For every supernatural gift that comes from God, satan has made a substitute. Ancient diviners foretold events by countless methods—from observing the inner parts of slaughtered sheep or goats to examining the patterns of drops of oil falling into a cup of water. Persons called *oracles* interpreted these so-called messages from the gods.

Over the centuries, there have been many attempts to stamp out satanic worship and witchcraft—some of them misguided and none completely effective. In the 1600s, suspected witches were tied up and thrown into the water. Those who sank were considered innocent. Those who floated were considered to be witches—and were burned at the stake or hanged.

It seems nothing has changed. Palm-reader and fortune-teller signs dot the landscape of the nation. Thousands of people are involved in dream interpretation, necromancy (communicating with the spirits of the dead), tarot card reading, voodoo, and astrology.

Former First Lady Nancy Reagan made headlines when it was learned that she consulted an astrologer in San Francisco to determine what days her husband should not fly in an airplane. Members of England's royal family have traveled to India to meet with gurus.

It is shocking to turn on a television set and see a famous Hollywood celebrity promoting a "psychic hot line." For two dollars a minute you can make a phone call and hear a tape recording that will supposedly reveal your future. The number should be 1-900-666-6666.

Why are people calling? Because mankind is crying out for a revelation from above—regardless of what kind of a god it is from.

When you listen to sorcerers, fortune-tellers, and astrologers, you are only hearing satan's plan for your life. It may sound enticing, but it will lead you down a path of destruction. Remember the fortune-teller who told me that I would become famous for my music? That wasn't God's plan. It was satan's. The path toward becoming a famous musician nearly killed me.

When I had dinner with Larry King, he asked me a question about the prophet and the psychic. I told him the difference is that a psychic talks to the dead who are supposedly living, but I talk to the living who are dead.

Those who read God's Word and hear His voice, however, are receiving the message of a loving God. They learn who they are in Christ and what they can become in His Kingdom.

FRAUDULENT FAITH

What is divination? It is simply an imitation of the divine. Moses told the children of Israel:

There shall not be found among you anyone who makes his son or his daughter pass through the fire, or one who practices witchcraft, or a soothsayer, or one who interprets omens, or a sorcerer, or one who conjures spells, or a medium, or a spiritist, or one who calls up the dead (Deuteronomy 18:10-11).

Then he added:

For all who do these things are an abomination to the Lord (Deuteronomy 18:12).

Under the influence of darkness, people are lured into consulting the powers of darkness. This evil is put on the same level as rebellion against God. According to Scripture it leads to death.

Saul, the first king of Israel, "died for his unfaithfulness which he had committed against the Lord, because he did not keep the word of the Lord, and also because he consulted a medium for guidance" (1 Chron. 10:13).

It is satan's aim to substitute the influence of evil spirits for the authority of the voice of God.

DIVINE POWER

When Paul and Silas brought the message of Christ to Philippi, satan decided to disturb their efforts.

Now it happened, as we went to prayer, that a certain slave girl possessed with a spirit of divination met us, who brought her masters much profit by fortune-telling. This girl followed Paul and us, and cried out, saying, "These men are the servants of the Most High God, who proclaim to us the way of salvation (Acts 16:16-17).

Many people believe that when satan speaks, it will either be a lie or a direct confrontation. They think it will be easy to say, "Oh, that is the devil talking. Shut up and sit down."

But satan is much more subtle and sly. He knows that "death and life are in the power of the tongue" (Prov. 18:21), and he wants to deceive you with flattery.

In this case he used flattery and a spirit of exhibitionism in his attempt to control or manipulate the work of the Lord.

Some observers must have thought the girl was promoting the apostles when again and again she said, "These men are the servants of the Most High God, who proclaim to us the way of salvation." Were her words accurate? Yes. Did God say it? No. That was the difference.

Satan is in the business of harassment and torment.

And this she did for many days. But Paul, greatly annoyed, turned and said to the spirit, "I command you in the name of Jesus Christ to come out of her." And he came out that very hour (Acts 16:18).

Why did Paul stop her? He realized that the words spoken by this young woman would cause great damage to the church that was being established.

Accuracy does not guarantee that a person is truly a man or woman of God. The Lord may get your attention through a prophet who tells you where you live. But never forget that satan knows your name and address, too. The slave girl at Philippi was imitating the divine, and it turned to divination.

We should also be aware of flattery and adulation. We love to hear someone say, "You are special in the sight of God." But I would much rather have a prophet tell me about an area of my life that God wants me to correct or improve than be flattered. It is truth that will set us free.

The prophet Micah in the Old Testament warned against those who expound for personal gain.

> *Thus says the Lord concerning the prophets who make my people stray; who chant "Peace" while they chew with their teeth, but who prepare war against him who puts nothing into their mouths: "Therefore you shall have night without vision, and you shall have darkness without divination; the sun shall go down on the prophets, and the day shall be dark for them* (Micah 3:5-6).

It is tragic when men and women of the Lord no longer hear what the Spirit is saying but remember what the Spirit said in the past. They have no fresh revelation. Instead in their desperate attempt to appeal to the masses, they imitate the anointing and fall into the trap of divination. To hear an "old" word is like eating manna that is more than one day old. It is spoiled and stinks (see Exod. 16:20). God wants to teach us the difference between the truth that is encrusted in the tomb and the word that is emboldened in the womb.

TRUTH IN THE TOMB AND TRUTH IN THE WOMB

A promise is not as effective as the product. A *promise* lingers in our thoughts and minds but the *product* of that imagination is what will shift our lives and the lives of those around us. We are always living in some form of process and this spiritual process is the space between the promise and the product. The process of re-evaluating what was once considered godly practice will result in the rejection of a powerless tradition that has no application in our generation. Tradition is simply continuing the old franchise of the past but eventually that old franchise becomes irrelevant. Chained to tradition, the church will never be able to discover the creative forces they were meant to possess.

Louis Dupre, professor of Philosophy at Yale University, wrote that "*Christianity has become an historical factor subservient to a secular culture, instead of functioning as the creative power it once was.*"[1] It is clear that too much of Christianity has become absorbed by the culture, rather than functioning as the creative power of the culture. Let us become the creative power that is affecting the culture, rather than a polluted pool of boring nonsense that has no relevant word for a dying culture. There are enough people in the church to infiltrate and shift the whole course of our present culture. But first we must be willing to give up all that religious, traditional nonsense and allow ourselves to become God's creative word to the world.

We have to re-evaluate everything that we have considered sacred. There are some serious *sacred cows* that we have observed as holy and they are not! We need to let them out to pasture and move on. The present church is without life because we place value on past experiences that we just refuse to leave behind. We would rather make them into sacred things—which God deems

---

1.   http://www.crosscurrents.org/dupre.htm

an abomination. We think it's a beautiful thing, but it's over. When we make something sacred, it replaces creative truth.

There is a difference between *historic* truth and *creative* truth. *Truth in a tomb is not the same as truth in a womb.* It was truth at one time (maybe) and it had its effect but now it is in a tomb; it is not truth that is creative. It has no potential unless it was transferred into this hour by the power of the birth—which we now call re-birth. Creative truth is lacking in the church. We are all hanging on what we *used* to do rather than doing what we *should* do.

Every time I come to a platform, I do not know what we are going to sing. Do you know why? Because I do not want our team to be in a non-creative place where we sing the same old thing and we say the same old thing. It might be a comfortable place but it is not a spiritual place.

So I make the people—though it can get repetitious at times—get creative and suddenly God starts singing the song and He starts doing it through creative power. Historical truth is not as important as creative truth. Inside of you is a creativity to bring something forth—not re-invent the wheel, but to do something that has never been done before. It's called the power of invention.

I'm not belittling historical truth, but we have these tendencies to take truth and build these historical monuments out of past revelations. A pile of ashes is not as effective as a burning bush. A burning bush was very powerful but when it stopped burning, it was not powerful. God is mobile, not static. We are all hanging around a bunch of ashes when He is already going down to Egypt to do some miracles and set His people free. Some people like to stay there and try to keep the bush burning, but it was God's voice that made the bush burn. Now it's just a pile of ashes we're trying to keep going. It's not effective anymore because God isn't there anymore.

It brought truth, but it didn't motivate Moses to build a tabernacle there. He went down to Egypt and faced hell. Pharaoh mocked him over and over. The court magicians performed some of the same wonders he did by God's power.

It's not going to be easy when God says, "This is what happened at the revival fire but now the revival has come to an end. What are you going to do with what was deposited in you during that time?" It's a creative power.

Truth in a tomb is not truth in a womb! Truth resurrected has a whole lot more to say. In the name of the old, you will do greater things. Creative truth means you are going to do greater things than were done yesterday. Authors, poets, entertainers, musicians, presidents, senators are going to feel the kingdom in its dominion. It is time to go in!

We are missionaries to a foreign culture, not a foreign land. The church has been forced to be an exile in a Babylonian culture. We want to stay huddled in Jerusalem, but God allowed us to be taken out of the huddle—despised and hated. Jesus told His disciples to go into all the earth but there they were enjoying what God was doing in Jerusalem. He had to send persecution to scatter them into all the ends of the earth. We are living in exile in a culture that is presently controlling us. We are employees not employers. But we are called to invade that culture. We need a bunch of Daniels and Esthers who will reach up to heaven and bring down God's creative power in the midst of an alien culture and shift the balance of power toward the righteous.

The Bible calls divination an abomination. God told the children of Israel that "the person who turns after mediums and familiar spirits, to prostitute himself with them, I will set My face against that person and cut him off from his people" (Lev. 20:6).

SUDDEN DARKNESS

Saul and Barnabas traveled to Cyprus, and...

when they had gone through the island to Paphos, they found a certain sorcerer, a false prophet, a Jew whose name was Bar-Jesus, who was with the proconsul, Sergius Paulus, an intelligent man. This man called for Barnabas and Saul and sought to hear the word of God (Acts 13:6-7).

The proconsul was the Roman governor of the island.

But Elymas the sorcerer (for so his name is translated) withstood them [Barnabas and Saul], seeking to turn the proconsul away from the faith (Acts 13:8).

But it didn't work.

Then Saul, who also is called Paul, filled with the Holy Spirit, looked intently at him and said, "O full of all deceit and all fraud, you son of the devil, you enemy of all righteousness, will you not cease perverting the straight ways of the Lord? And now, indeed, the hand of the Lord is upon you, and you shall be blind, not seeing the sun for a time." And immediately a dark mist fell on him, and he went around seeking someone to lead him by the hand (Acts 13:9-11).

What was the political leader's response? "Then the proconsul believed" (Acts 13:12). The proconsul saw the judgment of God coming.

If we expect to see God's righteousness in the governments of the world, we need to have the boldness of Paul and express the utterance of God. He became the mouthpiece of the Lord on the earth.

Satan could not give Paul the power to pronounce judgment over Elymas the sorcerer. Only God has that power. And He spoke the word through one of His servants. Paul did not come as a teacher, but he gave the greatest illustrated lecture any man could give.

I recently heard a religious leader say, "We don't need signs and wonders. The Word is sufficient." The proconsul would not have believed if that manifestation had not taken place. It was a sign of authority. And God has given us that same capability—not to speak the word of blindness, but to be obedient to the voice of God so we can dispel the power of divination.

I believe the Kingdom will come through people like you and me who are committed to becoming His voice. But first we must realize that we have His divinity inside of us. People will ask, "Where is the Kingdom?" We can answer in the words of Jesus, "For indeed, the kingdom of God is within you" (Luke 17:21).

Out of the Fire

The Lord makes it possible to access His power at the time of our greatest need.

Paul said that he escaped from a shipwreck and swam to the shore of the island of Malta.

The natives showed us unusual kindness; for they kindled a fire and made us all welcome, because of the rain that was falling and because of the cold. But when Paul had gathered a bundle of sticks and laid them on the fire, a viper came out because of the heat, and fastened on his hand (Acts 28:2-3).

As the people gathered around the apostle and "saw the creature hanging from his hand, they said to one another, 'No doubt this man is a murderer, whom, though he has escaped the sea, yet justice does not allow to live'" (Acts 28:4).

But Paul had divine power. "He shook off the creature into the fire and suffered no harm" (Acts 28:5). The people hardly knew how to respond.

They were expecting that he would swell up or suddenly fall down dead. But after they had looked for a long time and saw no harm come to him, they changed their minds and said that he was a god (Acts 28:6).

Again, it is human nature for unbelievers to deify people who have power from God. It's an instinctive reaction.

For the next three days one of the leading citizens of the island, Publius, opened his home to Paul.

> *And it happened that the father of Publius lay sick of a fever and dysentery. Paul went in to him and prayed, and he laid his hands on him and healed him. So when this was done, the rest of those on the island who had diseases also came and were healed* (Acts 28:8-9).

As Paul departed, the people honored him in "many ways" and "provided such things as were necessary" (Acts 28:10).

No power on earth is able to overcome the children of the Lord. When we confront the powers of darkness, the Lord is there to shine His eternal light and confound our foes. Listen to His words:

> *I am the Lord, who makes all things, who stretches out the heavens all alone, who spreads abroad the earth by Myself; who frustrates the signs of the babblers, and drives diviners mad* (Isaiah 44:24-25).

A DIVINE INHERITANCE

Not only has God given us a divine nature and power, He has given us a divine inheritance. Paul reminded the Ephesians of this:

> *In Him you also trusted, after you heard the word of truth, the gospel of your salvation; in whom also, having believed, you were sealed with the Holy Spirit of promise, who is the guarantee of our* **inheritance** *until the redemption of the purchased possession, to the praise of His glory* (Ephesians 1:13-14, emphasis added).

He also prayed that the Ephesians would know "what is the hope of His calling, what are the riches of the glory of His *inheritance* in the saints" (Eph. 1:18, emphasis added).

Today when you pray, thank the Lord that inside your spirit dwells the divine nature of God, the divine power of God, and the divine inheritance of God.

CHAPTER EIGHT

WHO IS SPEAKING?

Late one night I was praying after experiencing a serious back problem that did not improve. The Lord said to me, "You have been defiled by divination."

When those words came to me, I was shocked because I did not believe that as a man of God I could be defiled by somebody else. I said, "Lord, what do You mean 'defiled by divination'?"

I knew that people could injure themselves by adulterous thoughts, lies, anger, pride, and lust, Scripture tells us:

> *Do not love the world or the things in the world. If anyone loves the world, the love of the Father is not in him. For all that is in the world—the lust of the flesh, the lust of the eyes, and the pride of life—is not of the Father but is of the world* (1 John 2:15-16).

"Lord, I have tried to overcome these things. How else can satan attack me?"

"He can do it through the power of words," answered the Lord.

As I opened the pages of Scripture, the Spirit showed me how people suffer when a satanic force, "a familiar spirit," speaks into their lives.

> *For the idols speak delusion; the diviners envision lies, and tell false dreams; they comfort in vain. Therefore the people*

*wend their way like sheep; they are in trouble because there is
no shepherd* (Zechariah 10:2).

*"Behold, I am against those who prophesy false dreams," says
the Lord, "and tell them, and cause My people to err by their
lies and by their recklessness. Yet I did not send them or command them; therefore they shall not profit this people at all,"
says the Lord* (Jeremiah 23:32).

Moses warned the people of Israel of the danger of
divination.

*Give no regard to mediums and familiar spirits; do not seek
after them, to be defiled by them: I am the Lord your God*
(Leviticus 19:31).

The word *defiled* comes from a Hebrew word that means "to
be foul, especially in a ceremonial or moral sense; to be contaminated." It's a very strong word, often used to indicate sexual
immorality or idol worship.

Moses was warning the people that words of prophecy that
are not from the Lord are as dangerous as idol worship and sexual sin.

SPOKEN BY A STRANGER

We need to be extremely careful about accepting what people say. The faith teaching that Christians have heard in recent
years says that we are to make a positive confession, and we
should. But we need to remember that other people's words can
affect us as well.

The potential for danger is greatest with those who come to
you on a personal basis. They are the ones who corner you after
a meeting or outside of the church with a "special word from
God" for you.

Defilement takes place when words of dishonor are placed
in your spirit—words that are proclaimed as being straight from

God, but they are far from it. What is spoken can cause serious harm to your family, your business, and your spiritual life.

THE DANGER OF DEFILEMENT

Something that is defiled is unclean, impure, or filthy. Satan knows that the Church is to be without "spot or wrinkle or any such thing, but that she should be holy and without blemish" (Eph. 5:27). The enemy never sleeps in his attempt to tarnish the Church through the power of deceitful words spoken from the mouths of false prophets.

If the person who attempts to prophesy over you has not been sent from God, then who has given him or her the word? A "familiar spirit" has. The real danger, then, is that you will be defiled—or contaminated—by whatever that person harbors in his or her life. It is sad to see people attempt to use the gifts of the Spirit without the approval or anointing of God.

The Bible lists three major causes of defilement:

1. *You can be defiled by a spirit of bitterness.*

The author of Hebrews wrote:

*Pursue peace with all people, and holiness, without which no one will see the Lord: looking carefully lest anyone fall short of the grace of God; lest any root of bitterness springing up cause trouble, and by this many become **defiled*** (Hebrews 12:14-15, emphasis added).

2. *You can be defiled by disobedience.*

In his letter to Titus, Paul said:

*To the pure all things are pure, but to those who are **defiled** and unbelieving nothing is pure; but even their mind and conscience are **defiled**. They profess to know God, but in works they deny Him, being abominable, disobedient, and disqualified for every good work"* (Titus 1:15-16, emphasis added).

God equates a person who is defiled with an unbeliever who may claim to know the Lord but whose actions—as a result of disobedience—will cause that person to be disqualified for service.

3. *You can be defiled by the tongue.*

The spoken word has the power to desecrate the entire body.

> *Even so the tongue is a little member and boasts great things. See how great a forest a little fire kindles! And the tongue is a fire, a world of iniquity. The tongue is so set among our members that it **defiles** the whole body, and sets on fire the course of nature; and it is set on fire by hell* (James 3:5-6, emphasis added).

Always be aware "lest satan should take advantage of us; for we are not ignorant of his devices" (2 Cor. 2:11).

When the Lord told me I had been defiled by divination, I was lying on my back, unable to walk. I had been to the hospital twice for surgery, and I finally cried out to God, "What is happening?"

God answered, "This is what happened: You were defiled by divination."

"When?"

"The day those people at the convention spoke over you."

I remembered the day. I was attending a convention, and a group of people who were self-proclaimed prophets gathered around me and prophesied. They were complete strangers to me.

I had never heard so many good words in my whole life. They prophesied that I was going to go to Cairo to speak to princes and sheiks in their tents. I think Queen Elizabeth even got in there somewhere. I was going to have houses in this country and houses in that country. I would be rich and have clothes and all of that.

When they finished speaking, I said to myself, *I'll just put that word aside on a little shelf in my heart.*

Who Is Speaking?

The Lord told me in the hospital, "Those people did not hear or see anything from Me. That was not My word. Therefore, you were defiled."

What I should have done was reject those messages immediately. When I finally broke the power of that defilement, we had complete freedom in our home, and my health was restored.

Can We Know?

How can we defend against defilement? By being sensitive to the spirit of a person's heart. Jesus said, "For out of the abundance of the heart the mouth speaks" (Matt. 12:34). In some cases words are spoken from the *lack* of abundance of the heart.

The most important thing is not what a person ways, but the condition of his innermost being. One of the gifts God has made available to us is the "discerning of spirits" (1 Cor. 12:10). It is a gift that should be operating through you.

More than once, when I have felt God's warning signs, I have stopped a person who was attempting to speak into my life. Otherwise, I would have been defiled.

On the other hand, it is easy to use the wrong measuring stick to judge people. They may have personalities that do not please you. Their exteriors may be angry or calm. Their voices may be loud or soft. But that is not what counts. The only question you need to ask is, What about their heart?

It is not necessary to live with a spirit of distrust. You don't have to act as God's detective, telling people, "Don't speak to me." The Lord expects us to use a loving spirit, offering gentleness and consideration in dealing with others.

After years of being involved in a prophetic ministry, I can tell instinctively whether or not a person has a heart that is yielded to the Lord. It is a spiritual perception that God allows all of us to develop.

Some people say, "I will wait to see what the person says or how he or she acts." But you may be misguided since everyone has faults and failures.

The words people speak spring from the heart to the tongue and then become the spoken word. We can look past the vocabulary, the grammar, the culture, and the accent. What flows from a person's heart is what truly affects us.

At a recent conference I spoke with a married couple who said, "Pray for us. We are having tremendous problems in our home and with our personal health." They said, "We just don't understand it. We have fasted and prayed. And we have fought the fight of faith."

Suddenly the Spirit of the Lord gave me a word for them. I felt led to say, "Tell me about something that was spoken over your life about two years ago." After they reflected on my question, they told me the time, the place and the person who had spoken a prophetic word to them. Ever since that moment, everything in their life had gone downhill.

"Where is that person now?" I wanted to know.

"Well, he is no longer in the ministry. In fact, I don't believe he is living for the Lord," the husband responded.

Defilement was brought to this couple through a person whose heart was not right. We rebuked that word over their lives, and they were set free. There was a wonderful turnaround in their lives.

YOU ARE THE TABERNACLE

God revealed Himself to the people of Israel at Mount Sinai. Later in the Old Testament we read that "the Lord dwells in Zion" (Joel 3:21). The move from Sinai to Zion served to change the Israelites from one dimension of law to another. There was greater freedom in their praise and worship, but it was still legalistic.

In Zion (or Jerusalem), God's earthly presence was concentrated in one specific place—a tent. David "prepared a place for the ark of God, and pitched a tent for it" (1 Chron. 15:1).

When Christ came to earth and was crucified for sin, God allowed man to enter a new dimension. Now the Lord no longer dwells in an ark, a tent or a physical tabernacle that is thousands of miles away from us. We don't have to travel to the Holy Land to find God. He resides in you and me. We are His dwelling place. And that is the joy of the new covenant.

We have been given the right "to enter the Holiest by the blood of Jesus, by a new and living way which He consecrated for us" (Heb. 10:19-20). The Bible says we are now the house (Heb. 3:6), the tabernacle, and the temple.

Scripture declares:

For you are the temple of the living God. As God has said: I will dwell in them and walk among them. I will be their God, and they shall be My people (2 Corinthians 6:16).

Because of what Christ made possible, we have a great responsibility. In Old Testament times the priests were accountable for what entered the sanctuary. But now *we* are the sanctuary and are answerable for what enters *our* lives.

As Christians, our bodies are no longer our possessions. They have been bought with a price and are the temples of Almighty God. When you fully understand the sacred trust the Lord has placed in your care, you will protect and cherish your body with your very life. You will not allow anything that does not belong to enter the door of the sanctuary.

The Lord is so jealous of this habitation that He will judge anyone who defiles it—whether it is you or someone else.

Do you not know that you are the temple of God and that the Spirit of God dwells in you? If anyone defiles the temple of God, God will destroy him. For the temple of God is holy, which temple you are (1 Corinthians 3:16-17).

The tabernacle God has given you is not made by hands. It is a gift from on high.

> *Your body is the temple of the Holy Spirit who is in you, whom you have from God and you are not your own* (1 Corinthians 6:19).

The Lord's desire is to place a wall of protection around us to prepare us for the great day that is coming.

Once, when Jesus was crossing the Sea of Galilee with His disciples, a great windstorm arose.

> *The waves beat into the boat, so that it was already filling, but He was in the stern, asleep on a pillow. And they awoke Him and said to Him, "Teacher, do You not care that we are perishing?" Then He arose and rebuked the wind, and said to the sea, "Peace, be still!" And the wind ceased and there was a great calm. But He said to them, "Why are you so fearful? How is it that you have no faith?"* (Mark 4:37-40).

When you are in God's perfect will, you have no reason to be afraid. Your own will can fall victim to the devil's intimidation and control, but you can't be swayed when you're in the will of God. Remember, Christ gave Himself for our sins "that He might deliver us from this present evil age, according to the will of our God and Father" (Gal. 1:4). Why would He do that? Because it is only when you are out of God's will that satan can destroy you.

And the evil one wants to snatch you from the Father's will. He may attempt to do it by giving you a word through a false prophet to lead you in the wrong direction.

THE TWO TEMPLES

There are two types of temples spoken about in the New Testament. The Greek word *hieron* is used to describe the entire temple structure including the outer court—the physical building that is the house of God. But the word *naos* is used to describe the inner sanctuary of the temple which only priests could enter. Metaphorically, naos refers to the inner sanctuary of our hearts. It says in First Corinthians 6:19 (NIV), "Do you not know that your body is a temple [naos] of the Holy Spirit, who is in you?"

When Jesus went to the temple at Jerusalem, He was appalled to find people selling cattle, sheep, and doves—even exchanging money in such a holy place. Scripture records His response.

> *When He had made a whip of cords, He drove them all out of the temple, with the sheep and the oxen, and poured out the changers' money and overturned the tables* (John 2:15).

The temple He entered was the *hieron*—the building made of stone and mortar. He said "Take these things away! Do not make My Father's house a house of merchandise!" (John 2:16).

The Pharisees challenged the Lord and asked, "What sign do You show to us, since You do these things?"

Jesus answered, "Destroy this temple, and in three days I will raise it up" (John 2:18-19).

They did not understand that the *naos* Jesus referred to was not the physical building in which they were standing. The Jews then said: " 'It has taken forty-six years to build this temple, and will You raise it up in three days?' But He was speaking of the temple of His body" (John 2:20-21).

Jesus was trying to tell them, "I am the inner sanctuary of the Father. I am the glory of God. If you destroy this glory, in three days it will be raised up."

They had no idea that the Lord's words would be fulfilled by His crucifixion and resurrection.

We are not Christ on the earth, but His Spirit resides in our temple of flesh and blood. That is why God told Paul to instruct the people to guard the temple against defilement. We are the glory of the Lord and His sanctuary on earth.

FOREIGNERS NOT ALLOWED!

Since we are the temple of the Lord, we need to observe the principles found in the temple ordinances. Ezekiel talked a great deal about our responsibilities in this. The Lord brought Ezekiel to the temple and told him:

> *Son of man, mark well, see with your eyes and hear with your ears, all that I say to you concerning all the ordinances of the house of the Lord and all its laws. Mark well who may enter the house and all who go out from the sanctuary* (Ezekiel 44:5).

God was saying, "Pay close attention to those who would enter your temple—the dwelling place of the Most High." The Lord gave this commandment because each time someone speaks into your life, he or she is entering your sanctuary. If someone is not qualified to enter, turn that person away. God's word to Ezekiel was:

> *Say to the rebellious, to the house of Israel, "Thus says the Lord God: 'O house of Israel, let Us have no more of all your abominations. When you brought in foreigners, uncircumcised in heart and uncircumcised in flesh, to be in My sanctuary to defile it—My house—and when you offered My food, the fat and the blood, then they broke My covenant because of all your abominations'"* (Ezekiel 44:6-7).

The people were guilty of allowing "foreigners"—those whose hearts were not right with God—to enter the sanctuary and defile it.

Some immediate signs of not being in covenant with the Lord are having no horizontal covenantal relationship and no "covering"—no one to whom to be accountable. People who operate like this have independent ministries without the oversight of local churches. The Bible speaks of this type of person as "uncircumcised."

God is looking for people who are in covenant with the Word, with ministry leadership, with His church, and with Him. When we have made a pact with the Lord, we should be ready to become open before both God and man.

The Lord said through Ezekiel:

"You have not kept charge of My holy things, but you have set others to keep charge of My sanctuary for you." Thus says the Lord God: "No foreigner, uncircumcised in heart or uncircumcised in flesh, shall enter My sanctuary, including any foreigner who is among the children of Israel" (Ezekiel 44:8-9).

Centuries later, Paul told the church at Ephesus the good news that, as Christians, we are no longer from an alien country.

WHO CAN SPEAK?

You may be saying, "I understand that I am not allowed to have a foreigner enter my sanctuary. But who *is* allowed to speak into my life?"

Ezekiel allowed three categories of people to enter the temple.

But the priests, the Levites, the sons of Zadok, who kept charge of My sanctuary when the children of Israel went astray from Me...They shall enter My sanctuary, and they shall come near My table to minister to Me, and they shall keep My charge (Ezekiel 44:15-16).

A *priest* is someone who is set apart and consecrated to be engaged in holy matters. God tells us not to allow someone who is not anointed by the Lord to speak over our lives.

Unfortunately, it is rare for people to pause and reflect on a prophetic word they are receiving. They see someone operating in the gifts of the Spirit and are in awe of what is happening. Then they quickly call their friends and exclaim, "You should hear the amazing things this person is saying." They give practically no attention to the issues of anointing, righteousness, and commitment to the Lord.

Jesus said that you can identify false prophets "by their fruits" (Matt. 7:16).

> *And Aaron cast down his rod before Pharaoh and before his servants, and it became a serpent. But Pharaoh also called the wise men and the sorcerers; so the magicians of Egypt, they also did in like manner with their enchantments* (Exodus 7:10-11).

Through trickery, the king's wizards imitated God's miracle. But the Lord had the final word. Do you recall what happened to the sorcerers' snakes? Aaron's snake swallowed all of their snakes (see Exod. 7:12).

Often the results of a prophetic word cannot be determined when the seed is planted, but when the harvest comes. It is only natural to get excited when God's Spirit moves in a meeting. But I continue to tell people, "Don't judge my ministry by what happens in a particular service. Call me in two or three months—or even in one year." After some time passes, then we can really know what took place as a result of hearing God's voice.

A GREAT DAY COMING

The Lord tells us that those who will reign with Him are people whose garments have not been defiled (see Rev. 3:3-4). What is the reward for the overcomer? "He...shall be clothed in white garments, and I will not blot out his name from the Book of Life; but I will confess his name before My Father and before His angels" (Rev. 3:5).

We are fast approaching the hour that has been described as the conflict of the ages. Without question we are going to see the things of the Lord being duplicated by false apostles, false teachers, and false prophets as never before.

At the same time we will see a victorious outburst of God's expression on the earth—and you and I will participate in it. Truth will swallow up evil. The power of God will be unprecedented, and we will be ushered into a land that knows no defilement.

We will also hear the voice of God as He says, "Well done."

CHAPTER NINE

IF YOU ONLY KNEW

During a gathering in Rhode Island, I noticed a young man in the audience with his arms crossed, and he was frowning. I could tell that he was suffering from a disease that affected his face.

I felt led to walk over to him because God was directing me to those who were unsaved. He was a handsome young man despite his obvious health problems. When I asked him to stand, he rose reluctantly. I could see that he was extremely weak.

Then God gave me a prophetic word concerning some specific things about his life.

I said, "Opportunity stands at your door. You have a choice. 'If you will turn to God, He will raise you up, heal your bones, and make something of your life. You will live to tell the world of His name.'"

That message clearly surprised the young man.

I spoke with some of his relatives after the meeting. I learned that he was dying of a rare type of bone cancer and had only months to live. His relatives had convinced him to travel all the way from California to attend the meeting. I also was told that he was a rebellious young man who wanted little to do with Jesus. All of his past religious experiences had been disappointing.

A person with the gift of healing would have laid hands on him for an instant miracle. But I was there to deliver a prophetic word from the Lord. Each one of God's gifts is unique.

The young man did not receive salvation during that meeting. I had given him the word of the Lord. Now it was up to him to accept or reject God's call.

NO PRECONDITIONS

When Jesus told His disciples to perform miracles in His name, He didn't say, "Ask them if they are believers. See if they know the doctrines of the church."

Jesus simply said, "Heal the sick, cleanse the lepers, raise the dead, cast out demons. Freely you have received, freely give" (Matt. 10:8). He told the disciples, "Heal the sick there, and say to them, 'The kingdom of God has come near to you'" (Luke 10:9). There were no preconditions to Christ's healing power. In fact, I believe God allows miracles to happen so people will be convinced of His love.

Jesus did not say the Kingdom of God would be *upon* them. He said it was *near* them. When God is present, He offers the opportunity for someone to enter the Kingdom.

When that young man in Rhode Island sat down, he was not suddenly free of cancer. But he left that meeting with a new idea about who Jesus was. He realized that even in his pathetic state, God was concerned enough to speak to him.

> *See that you do not refuse Him who speaks. For if they did not escape who refused Him who spoke on earth, much more shall we not escape if we turn away from Him who speaks from heaven* (Hebrews 12:25).

The next day the young man told his sister, "I want Jesus."

"Let's pray together," she said. As the two of them prayed, he surrendered his heart.

That night he attended once again, now a transformed young man. The scowl was gone. He was lifting his hands and celebrating his salvation—and he had been physically healed as well.

What Do You Expect?

You only have to read a few pages of the Bible to know that God's ways are never dull and boring. He rarely accomplishes His purpose through repetition. Instead, His commandments and promises are always fresh.

In fact, His ways are so unique that some people do not even know the Lord is speaking to them. That's how it was when Jesus spoke to the woman at the well.

As far as she was concerned, the man conversing with her was a total stranger. She said, " 'How is it that You, being a Jew, ask a drink from me, a Samaritan woman?' For Jews have no dealings with Samaritans" (John 4:9).

Jesus answered her, "If you knew the gift of God, and who it is who says to you, 'Give Me a drink,' you would have asked Him, and He would have given you living water" (John 4:10).

The Lord was encouraging the woman to ask questions, saying, in effect, "If you only knew what was available, you would begin to ask, and the Father would begin to give." If she had only known it was Jesus, she could have had "living water."

If people could just comprehend, they would ask and receive. They would seek and find. They would knock and the door would be opened. We need to absorb as much knowledge as possible concerning what the Lord has in His storehouse— whether it is about healing, wisdom, prophecy, or the other gifts of the Spirit.

A River Problem

Would you settle for something you expect to hear rather than let God give you something you thought was impossible?

His word may not be what you imagine. He may not even address the issue that's facing you at the moment.

That's what happened to Naaman, the commander of the Syrian army, a mighty man of valor—and a leper. A young girl from Israel who was a servant to Naaman's wife had said, "If only my master were with the prophet who is in Samaria! For he would heal him of his leprosy" (2 Kings 5:3).

So Naaman went to the king of Israel, who told him how to get to the prophet Elisha's house.

Than Naaman went with his horses and chariot, and he stood at the door of Elisha's house. And Elisha sent a messenger to him, saying, "Go and wash in the Jordan seven times, and your flesh shall be restored to you, and you shall be clean" (2 Kings 5:9-10).

That is not what Naaman imagined he would hear. When this proud pagan reached the home of the prophet, he believed he knew exactly how this man would perform the miracle. He had the scenario scripted perfectly. When his expectations weren't met, Naaman became furious and went away, saying:

Indeed, I said to myself, "He will surely come out to me, and stand and call on the name of the Lord his God, and wave his hand over the place, and heal the leprosy" (2 Kings 5:11).

He became even more incensed at the thought of washing in Israel's Jordan River. So he turned and went away in a rage. His servants encouraged Naaman to try what Elisha had commanded. When he did, "his flesh was restored like the flesh of a little child, and he was clean" (2 Kings 5:14).

The instruction given by Elisha demonstrated to Naaman that his healing would not come from the purity of the water, but from the power of the God of Israel. But he received only because he obeyed the prophet.

He ran back to Elisha and said, "Indeed, now I know that there is no God in all the earth, except in Israel" (2 Kings 5:15).

That's the creative God we serve.

Why does the Lord give instructions as specific as those He gave to Naaman? God told Naaman exactly where he should go because that place—the Jordan River—became God's habitation at that point in time. If someone else had leprosy, went to the same river and dipped seventy or even seven hundred times, that person would not be healed.

You can't expect to live on the prophetic word given to someone else. The Lord gives unique, specific words. It is a private matter between you and God that cannot be reproduced.

Many people do not receive the promise for the same reason the world did not receive Jesus when He walked on the earth. Christ was the Living Word, but He did not conform to their expectations and guidelines.

They expected Him to follow Old Testament customs and behave in a strict, well-defined manner. They were shocked that a person who claimed to be the Son of God would not follow their regulations. But by refusing Jesus, they also rejected the Word. Two thousand years have passed, and the problem remains. When the voice of God speaks, most people fail to listen because of their preconceived notions of how God should respond. Then when God gives them an answer they don't want to hear, they immediately close their minds and hearts.

I am reminded of what happened after a meeting I conducted. The pastor took me aside and said, "Kim, that is not what our people expected to hear."

"I'm sorry you feel that way," I responded. Evidently, this pastor did not understand the difference between methods and principles.

METHODS VERSUS PRINCIPLES

We have our methods that might work once but the problem is that when somebody devises a method and it works we get lazy and we stick with that method. If all you are ever doing is learning the methods that worked for others then you will be tied to your methods. The repetition of methods creates laziness and lack of faith.

If you are tied to your method, it means that more than likely you do not believe God, but you believe your beliefs in God before you believe God, because your beliefs have a method that has worked. Therefore, it is so difficult to break away from that because it is a comfort zone, and God wants you to break away. If you are tied to your methods, it means that you are becoming religious.

You know that is still okay for a season, but there comes a point when you must realize that you have got to learn the principles. The principles in the Word are what work. Sometimes we love the book of the Lord more than we love the Lord of the book. You may not understand this, but I tell you, you can worship the Bible more than you actually worship God. You can worship your beliefs more than you worship God.

It is easier and more comfortable, to operate when locked into your beliefs. But God wants you to break out of that, and learn principles for yourself, and once you have learned the principles in the Bible you can devise your own methods that will begin to work for you. Principles are the foundations of the methods. If you never learn the principle then you will always be tied to a meaningless method. There is a generation that is saying, "You know what, those methods worked 50 years ago, but they don't work now!"

The church has been using the same methods of preaching and worship for years, but now individuals are rising up here and there saying, "You know what, I am going to devise my own methods using the same principle." The principle will always work even though the methods may change. It is going to give somebody else a way to get to the cross, into the Kingdom, and into the will of God. Principles never change but methods will always be changing.

If you are thinking, "I want to get into the Kingdom of God," then this is what you have to do. You have got to find the principle, and see what God does. He gives you a word, and says "Now listen." How many of you have read the Word and know that it works? You know the Word works. God gave us the Word, which contains principles that work.

Prophecy is the method that God gives you to make the "word" work. When God gives you a word, He then says, "Now find a method in which this word or this principle can work." In your action to the prophetic word you will discover the creative power of God acting on your behalf.

Time for Action

God is able to speak miracles into your life, but don't presume that He will always act alone. He will probably demand action on your part.

In Jerusalem during the time of Christ, a pool called Bethesda was located by the Sheep Gate. Every day it attracted "a great multitude of sick people, blind, lame, paralyzed, waiting for the moving of the water" (John 5:3).

They believed that an angel came to the pool at certain times and stirred up the water. Then whoever stepped in the pool first was made whole.

Now a certain man was there who had an infirmity thirty-eight years. When Jesus saw him lying there, and knew that he already had been in that condition a long time, He said to him, "Do you want to be made well?" (John 5:5-6).

Why did Jesus ask the man such an obvious question? Of course he wanted to be healed! Christ knew both the man's physical ailment and the condition of his heart. But He wanted to see the man respond to his need—to take the initiative that would result in his healing.

The sick man answered Him, "Sir, I have no man to put me into the pool when the water is stirred up; but while I am coming, another steps down before me" (John 5:7).

For 38 years he waited for someone else to come and help him. He was saying, "I have no one to do it for me." He didn't realize that the miracle was not in the water, but rather, it was in responding to the voice of the Lord.

Jesus said to him, "Rise, take up your bed and walk." And immediately the man was made well, took up his bed, and walked (John 5:8-9).

The Lord wants us to be in divine communication with Him. Once that happens, we can expect Him to intercede on our behalf.

Our relationship must be directly with the Father, not through a second or third party. We just need to say, "Lord, I'm in an impossible situation. Tell me what to do." Nothing compares with specific direction from the Lord.

What was the lesson God taught at the pool of Bethesda? Don't expect God to move unless you take the first step yourself.

In most instances, Christ's miracles were accompanied by a command to do something specific. He often healed people through His sovereign touch or through His spoken word, but most of the time, He would also give them a directive, such as "rise up," "walk," or "wash your eyes."

Here is how Jesus asked people to put their faith into action.

- To the man with the withered hand at the synagogue, Jesus said, "Stretch out your hand" (Matt. 12:13). When he stretched it out, it was restored as whole as the other.
- When Jesus came to the ten lepers in Samaria, He told them, "Go show yourselves to the priests" (Luke 17:14).

As they were on their way to the priests, they were cleansed.

- To the nobleman whose son was close to death, He said, "Go your way; your son lives" (John 4:50). As the man was on his way home, his servants met him, saying that his son's fever was gone.

- When the disciples had fished all night and had caught nothing, He said, "Cast the net on the right side of the boat (John 21:6). They did, and they took in an incredible catch of fish.

- To the paralytic in Capernaum, He said, "Arise, take up your bed, and go to your house" (Mark 2:11). He arose immediately and obeyed, amazing the crowd.

- When He healed the leper in Jerusalem, He said, "Show yourself to the priest" (Matt. 8:4).

- To the man born blind, the Lord commanded, "Go, wash in the pool of Siloam" (John 9:7). The man did as Jesus commanded and returned with his sight.

Many people say, "I will wait for the Lord to come to me." They don't realize that as believers we have the incredible ability to come into His throne room at any time. But we need to take the first step and say, "Lord, I need to hear Your voice."

When I am driving down the highway, the air is filled with radio signals. But I am only able to hear the sounds when I turn on my radio. And it is that way with God's voice. When we open the channels of communication, the Lord can begin to accomplish His purpose.

MODULATION

I have learned through painful experiences that the first word I receive from the Lord is the one I must give. I can't second-guess God and turn to logic, intuition, or the circumstances of the moment. With total faith and reliance on Him, I must give what comes to my heart.

When God speaks, He only needs to do it once. Scripture tells what happened to one prophet who was disobedient to God's first instructions.

During the reign of King Jeroboam in Israel, a prophet left Judah and went to Bethel as God had instructed him. While the king stood before the sacred altar burning incense, the prophet cried out,

> *O altar, altar! Thus says the Lord: "Behold, a child, Josiah by name, shall be born to the house of David; and on you he shall sacrifice the priests of the high places who burn incense on you, and men's bones shall be burned on you"... This is the sign which the Lord has spoken: Surely the altar shall split apart, and the ashes on it shall be poured out* (1 Kings 13:2-3).

When King Jeroboam heard those words, he held out his hand and said, "Arrest him!" And the hand that he stretched out toward the prophet withered so that he couldn't even draw it back toward his body (see 1 Kings 13:4). Then, as was prophesied, the altar was split apart and the ashes were poured out.

Jeroboam immediately turned to the man of God and said, "Please entreat the favor of the Lord your God, and pray for me, that my hand may be restored to me" (1 Kings 13:6). The prophet prayed, and the king's hand was completely healed. Then Jeroboam said, "Come home with me and refresh yourself, and I will give you a reward" (1 Kings 13:7).

But God had told the prophet not to "eat bread, nor drink water, nor return by the same way you came" (1 Kings 13:9). So he refused the king's offer and left the city by another route.

But that wasn't the end of the story. As the prophet was returning home, he was met by an older prophet, who asked him to come to his home to eat. The young prophet refused again, explaining what God had commanded him to do.

Then came the test. The older prophet said to him,

I too am a prophet as you are, and an angel spoke to me by the word of the Lord, saying, "Bring him back with you to your house, that he may eat bread and drink water" (1 Kings 13:18).

The old prophet was lying, but the young prophet believed him. So he went back with him, and they ate and drank together.

Then, as they sat at the table, the word of the Lord came to the old prophet, and he cried out:

Thus says the Lord: "Because you have disobeyed the word of the Lord, and have not kept the commandment which the Lord your God commanded you...your corpse shall not come to the tomb of your fathers (1 Kings 13:21-22).

After the meal, the young man saddled his donkey and continued his journey home. On the journey, "a lion met him on the road and killed him" (1 Kings 13:24). When the old prophet heard what had happened, he said, "It is the man of God who was disobedient to the word of the Lord," and he mourned for him (1 Kings 13:26).

When you hear the unmistakable voice of God, never allow any man or woman—regardless of their credentials—to lead you astray. Your future does not depend on the alliance someone else has with God, but on *your* relationship with Him.

DON'T "SHELVE" IT

The voice of the Lord is not an obscure, clouded impression, but a clear and distinct sound. If you think it sounds good, but you are not sure it is God, then it probably *isn't* the Lord. You need to be aware that many false prophets can tell you many good things. But "good" is not always God.

Some people listen to a prophetic word or a teaching and say, "Well, if it is not from God, I will just file it. I'll put it on the shelf." As believers we should not "shelve" anything. We should act immediately to either receive the voice of God or reject a false message. Our decision should be based on whether or not the word is confirmed in your spirit.

False doctrine is simple to detect. You can turn to chapter and verse for a reference. But a prophet does not say, "According to Scripture I am giving you this word." He says, "Thus says the Lord," and you have to either accept it or turn it away.

In some cases you may remain in a quandary regarding the validity of a spoken word. Then you should pray earnestly for God's guidance. If you don't have peace in your heart, dismiss the message—regardless of who the prophet is.

People who do not know how the Spirit operates take a prophetic word and rush to presume what it means. Often they give their own interpretations, not God's. We need to slow down. If we hold on to what we receive, God will unfold it in His own time. Out of one revelation will spring another, then another, until the prophecy is fulfilled.

Those who become the voice of God are the watchmen of our day. But being a watchman carries with it a great burden. God told the prophet Ezekiel:

> *Son of man, speak to the children of your people, and say to them: "When [the watchman] sees the sword coming upon the land, if he blows the trumpet and warns the people, then whoever hears the sound of the trumpet and does not take warning, if the sword comes and takes him away, his blood shall be on his own head"* (Ezekiel 33:2-4).

But what happens if the watchman sees danger coming and fails to blow the trumpet?

> [If] *the sword comes and takes any person from among them, he is taken away in his iniquity; but his blood I will require at the watchman's hand* (Ezekiel 33:6).

When God gives you a word—whatever the message— proclaim it loud and clear.

WHEN PROPHECY FAILS

Some people seem surprised when I tell them, "Not everything a prophet says will happen." They have heard so many "name-it-and-claim-it" messages that they believe anything spoken by someone with a prophetic ministry will come to pass. But that is not always the case.

In these two specific instances, the voice of the Lord will not be fulfilled:

1. When people reject God's promise of hope and continue to live in their sins, God's word of blessing will not be fulfilled.

2. When people walk in disobedience to the logos (spoken) word and refuse to heed the commands of Christ.

Jonah was a chosen mouthpiece of God, but his prophecy did not come to pass. The Lord told him: "Arise, go to Nineveh, that great city, and cry out against it; for their wickedness has come up before Me" (Jon. 1:2).

The prophet fled from his mission and sailed for Tarshish. In the midst of a violent storm, he was thrown overboard and was swallowed by a great fish. Jonah repented and was thrown up on dry ground.

For the second time the voice of the Lord came and said, "Arise, go to Nineveh, that great city, and preach to it the message that I tell you." When he entered the city he cried out and said, "Yet forty days, and Nineveh shall be overthrown!" (Jon. 3:2,4).

But his prophecy did not happen. The people of Nineveh "believed God, proclaimed a fast, and put on sackcloth, from the greatest to the least of them" (Jon. 3:5).

The Lord saw that "they turned from their evil way; and God relented from the disaster that He had said He would bring upon them, and He did not do it" (Jon. 3:10). Nineveh's repentance canceled Jonah's prophetic word.

That scene is repeated many times in the Old Testament. God's spokesman pronounced havoc and calamity, but the people turned to the Lord and were spared.

At the cross, the prophet's message changed dramatically. The voice of the Lord became one of love, of hope and of promise. The word He now gives through His prophets—with few exceptions—is a bright and joyful sound.

PROPHECY IS A PROMISE

There are many reasons why a prophecy is not fulfilled. First, you must understand that a prophecy is a promise pertaining to the future, and when God speaks to a human being he is taking a risk because the human plays a part in the fulfillment of the promise.

I say that, because God has to deal with the will of man. As I previously explained, you cannot change a man's will by force. A human being may do that, but God never will. God is not a manipulator. He will encourage you to say yes to His will by offering you something better, the proverbial "carrot," but He will not force you against your will.

The revealed character of God shows us that with everybody He spoke to, He always brought the *end* into his or her beginning. He told Moses, "I'm going to deliver the people of Israel and take you to a land flowing with milk and honey." That's how He begins enticing you to do what you would consider a most difficult task. He shows you the glory of the end without always telling you about the process to get to that place.

When Joseph had a dream about his brothers bowing down before him, God was showing him he was going to be a king. But He didn't tell Joseph of the things that would happen before the fulfillment of that dream, as we all know. Joseph passed through the fire on the way to the fulfillment of God's word. If he had fallen into the trap set by Potiphar's wife, he would never have made it to that ultimate destiny he had seen in his dream. You may be saying to yourself, "Well, if God said it, He has to do it." No. God does not have to do anything, if you do not do your part. God shows you what could be and then gives you the power to enter into its reality, but you must take the first step of the journey.

Remember when Elijah complained to God that he was the only prophet left in the land, after he had challenged the Baal prophets in First Kings 19:14-18? God said to him, "I have in reserve 7,000 other prophets." This tells me that God had thousands of others in place that would have been able to do this job, even though He believed Elijah could do it. God always has a reserve, but it's not His best, His first choice. It's not what He wants to use. God will accomplish His purposes, even if we fail, but it is always His desire that we enter into the joy of "mission accomplished."

When He spoke to Jonah about Nineveh and Jonah was disobedient and ran away, God used a certain amount of intimidation with him. God does have his "ways and means" committee that will put pressure on us to respond to His word. Well, a fish swallowed Jonah, but remember this, Jonah decided to jump into the stormy waters because he didn't want the sailors who were on that ship to die. He offered himself so they wouldn't die, which was a beautiful type of Christ. So God allowed him to live because of his changed heart, and he was allowed to go to Nineveh to complete his divine mission. Because of his obedience, a whole city and nation was saved.

NOT ALL PROPHETIC WORDS COME TO PASS

There are many examples of God saying something that doesn't come to pass. Let me give you an example from Isaiah 38. When Isaiah was the prophet in the land of Israel, God gave him a word for Hezekiah who was king at that time. He said, "Go tell Hezekiah that he must set his house in order for he shall surely die." After Isaiah leaves, the king falls on his face and begs

God to forgive him, saying, "God, I'm going to remind You of all the things I've done, that I've tried to do for You, and I want to live." And before Isaiah even made it out of the king's palace, God says to him, "Turn around, go back and tell King Hezekiah I have added 15 years to his life."

Now don't tell me that God didn't change His mind. He did! God speaks to you as if you were going to do His biding, as if you were going to be obedient, as if you were going to do everything to comply to make that word come to pass. A lot of people say, "Well, God said that I will be healed, and I'm getting worse," or "God said my brother would live and he died!"

Prophecy doesn't have to say to somebody, "You will live." The Bible says that you have life or death in front of you and that you are to choose this day. So there's a choice! "I am the Lord your God that heals you." The Scriptures say that by His stripes you will be healed. In the Covenant today, we have a promise from God, even without it being prophetically stated that you can be healed. When a prophet says to someone, "I have healed you," or "I will heal you," it is the intention of God to do such a thing. Now, your actions can reverse that promise.

Someone says, "My brother was given a prophecy that he would live. He had cancer and he died." Nevertheless, it was God's intention to heal him. God's Word says, "I am the Lord God that heals you." Under the New Covenant, your covenant privileges include healing, deliverance, and salvation. Ultimately, death has no sting and the grave has no victory. There is no sting in death because of Christ.

When Eli the priest was chosen by God, we're told that God had chosen Eli and his family to be the priests for generations to come (see Exod. 29:9). However, Eli had allowed his sons to bring corruption into the temple. They were sleeping with the women who came to worship. They stole from the offerings and sacrifices that were brought to the temple. Eli did nothing about it as a father. As the high priest, he had a serious responsibility to keep the temple clean and he failed to do that. Therefore, the One who chose Eli must now look for a new prophetic priest.

One day, a prophet came on the scene and gave Eli a word from God, "I did say that I have chosen you and your family to be priests for generations to come, but now I say you shall be cut off" (see 1 Sam. 2:27-36). Now that is something we cannot ignore! God had told Eli that he was going to be priest for generations to come, but God changed His mind—not because He wanted to, but because Eli had changed his disposition and walk with God. He became lazy and overweight, which speaks of a spiritual truth. Eli just couldn't be bothered. He allowed corruption to come into his family and into the temple. So God said, "You're not the one anymore."

Samuel was accredited by God and given the honor that "not one of Samuel's words would fall to the ground" (see 1 Sam. 3:19). That was true up to a point, however. When Samuel prophesied over Saul to be the king of Israel, he said, "I have anointed you to be the commander of Israel." Samuel prophesied that great word, but Saul did not act according to the rules and did not comply. God then said, "I have chosen Myself another man" (see 1 Sam. 15:28). Of course, we know that was David.

YOUR FACE IS IN YOUR FUTURE

The Lord in a night vision approached Ananias; he was told to go to Strait street and pray for a man by the name of Saul. His first response was, "'Lord, he has power to bind and kill the Christians." He could have, at that point, said, "I'm not going." Jesus, however, had made an important statement to him. He had said, "You must go, Ananias, because I have already shown Saul your face" (see Acts 9:10-14).

Jesus was saying, "Your face, your person, is already in the future. I've already shown Saul that you are the man who is going to deliver him from his blindness. What will happen if you don't go?" I believe that God speaks His word to each person with the full intention of accomplishing it, but then, from that point onward, it is that person's responsibility to comply with the conditions that are set in the Bible.

In other words, if I look at someone and say, "The Lord is going to heal you and you're going to do this and do that, and have two children," that's the word of the Lord. I don't have to say in that prophecy, "but you have to obey the rules. You must love your brothers and not have unforgiveness in your heart. You must do this and do that." You don't have to be told certain *rules* that are already in the Bible.

When God speaks to you, He's assuming (I say *assuming* lightly) that you already know the conditions because they're already in His revealed word, the Bible. Let's say I said to somebody, "God is going to give you two children. You're going to have a happy marriage. You're going to have two businesses and you're going to move to Phoenix, Arizona."

That's a good prophecy! Let's say I'm prophesying to a couple and the man decides he doesn't want to be with his wife anymore, so he goes off with another woman. He breaks the rules that apply to that prophetic word, and it is immediately brought to nothing because of his act. Now God can still fulfill that word for his wife, because a promise remains.

"There remaineth therefore a rest to the people of God. For he that is entered into his rest, he also hath ceased from his own works, as God did from His. Let us labour therefore to enter into that rest, lest any man fall after the same example of unbelief" (Heb. 4:9-11 KJV). The word *remains* means it is still available. The word never comes back to God until it has accomplished that which it was sent out to do. So the conditions apply to the human being. God does not do it Himself. He needs your cooperation. You have to comply, and you have to work with Him. You have to labor to enter into the promise He has given you. You have to walk in the spirit. You have to obey the rules and commandments of Jesus Christ.

If I look at a man and say, "You have AIDS; but you will live and not die," that man could still die. He could walk out of that meeting and say, "I don't believe this. I don't think I can do this."

I once prophesied over a man in San Francisco who had AIDS and told him that the Lord was healing him that night and that he would live. He would go and speak to gays by the tens of thousands. The doctor had given him a few months to live, but he took that prophetic word and applied it to his life and received that promise. He lived for eight and a half years. He went to Russia during that time and spoke to thousands of gays at a gay convention. He sang and told them about Jesus Christ and thousands of them became believers and got freed. The prophecy was fulfilled though he did die less than nine years after receiving it.

Later when I was confronted about it, I said, "First of all, he was supposed to be dead in a few months, yet it was over eight years before he died. Just before dying, he said, 'The only father that I've ever had has been Kim Clement, the prophet who gave me this word, because he watched over me and he prayed for me and he stood with me.'" He did not die in defeat. The point I'm trying to make is that death is not a victory over God. Everything spoken prophetically was fulfilled during that man's life.

FAITH AND THE PROPHETIC WORD

There are conditions of faith. Faith has to be applied when you have a prophecy given to you. Sight has to be applied as you keep the vision in front of you. The enemy will try to steal your perception, because when God gives you a prophetic word you have immediately been given a vision. And if that vision is clouded and you cannot see anymore, and start stumbling around in the dark, you lose faith. If you lose sight and vision, you lose the promise. It's easy to blame somebody else and it's easy to say the word didn't come to pass because the prophet was a false prophet.

There's a condition in Luke and another in Malachi that illustrates our point.

> *Give, and it shall be given unto you; good measure, pressed down, and shaken together, and running over, shall men give into your bosom. For with the same measure that ye mete withal it shall be measured to you again* (Luke 6:38 KJV).

> *Bring ye all the tithes into the storehouse, that there may be meat in Mine house, and prove Me now herewith, saith the Lord of hosts, if I will not open you the windows of heaven, and pour you out a blessing, that there shall not be room enough to receive it* (Malachi 3:10 KJV).

The act of giving releases heavenly forces that will bring blessing into your life. The blessings are there. They are a promise to you, but the key that opens the door is in your hands and can only be opened by you.

In Hebrews 4 it says that the children of Israel were not able to enter the land or enter the rest because of unbelief. Do you realize that God had promised Moses and promised the children of Israel that at that point they would go into the Promised Land and they didn't? Forty years later, another generation would go with Joshua.

I'm trying to show you today that when a prophecy does not come to pass, 99 percent of the time it's based on people's reactions and their responses: faith, vision, and compliance with what the Scripture lays down. You choose. Now there are times when a prophet can make a mistake, and I have no problem saying that just like anybody else I can make a mistake. However, there are many factors that keep a word from finding its place of fulfillment. It is not always easy to know why.

Do you recall in Joshua where God had said, "Go in, take all the nations, possess the land, for I've put it in your hand, if you do not fear"? In other words, in every nation that you go into and fight you will experience victory, but you cannot have fear.

Joshua is having one victory after the other, and then they come to a town called Ai. Joshua is so confident in God's promise that he sends a few thousand soldiers in to fight the city of Ai. However, there was a condition God said to them, "When you go into these lands I do not want you to take possession of the accursed thing." This word could be considered in modern terminology as "banned substances" when He was talking about "the accursed thing." Upon entering into the city of Jericho, Achan came upon a "Babylonian garment," 200 shekels of silver, and a wedge of gold weighing 50 shekels, and he desired them. Thus he took these things and buried them in the dirt in his tent. He had taken of the divinely banned substance and he knew better. This act of defiance would affect Israel as they marched toward Ai.

One man's action brought about corruption and that corruption brought about a defeat for Israel. God's promise of victory was thwarted because of the treasonous action of Achan. Joshua was very angry because of the defeat, and, not realizing Achan's actions, he said to God, "You made a promise to me." And God said, "No, someone has taken of the accursed thing. Make things right and the promise will be yours."

I have gone to great lengths on this issue in order that you might understand that a prophetic promise can disappear in the darkness of human actions. If we take banned substances or violate God's word, we will run the risk of losing the promise. The only way back is through the door of obedience.

PROPHETS AND FALSE PROPHETS

The unmistakable difference between God's prophet and a false prophet is this: God's spokesman only knows God's plan for your life; the fraudulent seer only knows the human desire of man.

I become greatly concerned when people speak a word of destruction. For example, someone may make a great pronouncement such as, "There is going to be an earthquake on March 23." Ask yourself if that is an act of God or of satan.

God may know what the devil is going to do, but He certainly is not satan's mouthpiece. Instead, the voice of God is sent to reveal the plan of the Father for your life. He may show you where you are going wrong, but He will guide you to a path of safety. He prophesies *goodness*.

It is through God's voice that we can have a glimpse of the great things He has planned.

CHAPTER TEN

HOPE EQUALS INSIGHT AND FORESIGHT

Fear grips the hearts of those who cannot see the future. It is this sense of angst and uncertainty that feeds our fears. If we can see into the future, then maybe this will inspire hope. In fact, trying to see the future has always been a goal of humankind. We believe that if we can see into the future our fears will be silenced and we will discover hope and courage. There are two ways to *see* the future, and they are through insight and foresight.

Insight has to do with your field of vision, and this vision is made possible by something other than our five senses. It is an extension of sight and the capacity to discern the true nature of a situation, grasping the inward or hidden nature of things by an intuitive manner.

Paul prayed that the Ephesian church would experience this insightful power when he prayed that, "...the eyes of your understanding being enlightened; that ye may know what is the hope of His calling, and what the riches of the glory of His inheritance in the saints" (Eph. 1:18 KJV). Insight is the ability to know certain things because you have a new set of eyes for the invisible, seeing things that others do not see.

Foresight is the ability to perceive and identify events before they occur. It is the discovery and distinguishing of the nature of events before they have come into existence. It is the ability to *look forward* in time.

Hope is transformed into a reality by the power of insight and foresight. Insight and foresight are only possible when we receive the ability to *see* through the Spirit's eyes. Most people don't realize that we are controlled with a natural field of vision. We measure all things according to what we see with our natural eyes. We also measure danger according to what we see. We measure distance and drive cars and take walks by the power of our natural field of vision. Our natural vision and hearing have controlled us for way too long. We must be freed from our spiritual blindness and vision impairment. As children of God we are called to walk by faith, not by sight. Faith gives us the new set of eyes to be able to see what others do not see.

Prophetic vision offers no selfish desire. God does not lure you with desire without knowledge. He gives you knowledge, which then instigates desire. If you are controlled by desire when it comes to prophetic vision, you are definitely not going to fulfill something incredible. The prophetic is not for the curious, but for the committed, for those who are committed to respond to what they see.

When God gives you prophetic vision, sometimes there is no desire there to start with. However, the prophetic awakens desire. Those who pursue the prophetic out of uncontrolled desire are dangerous to the Kingdom. They have no knowledge of the true purpose of the prophetic, which is to serve God and others, not your own selfish needs and desires. A guy who is pursuing a girl just because he wants her will go to any lengths to try and impress her, because there is desire driven without knowledge. True love is born out of knowledge of the person and it is this knowledge that is the birthplace of desire.

If you truly want to be a prophetic person and if you truly want to be a complete person and go further than you are now, then you must be completed in this one thing. You have to be blind or you have to lose your sight to get insight. You have to lose sight of yourself so that you can see in a brand-new way. To see outward you have to take your eyes off of yourself.

You gotta get outta sight to get insight and you gotta get insight to get foresight. Most people don't even know what that means. Sight is your natural field of vision that you are controlled by but to be able to see with spiritual eyes you have to turn from the normal way of seeing.

When you get insight, you are no longer controlled by your natural field of vision. You are not controlled by what you see or what you hear. You are not controlled by what is happening in front of you. You are not controlled by what is happening or controlled by what you hear on the phone or the news. That's sight. You have got to get outta sight to get insight.

Insight means that you are only controlled by the true nature of the situation. You have looked beyond the natural. You've looked beyond what you have seen, and now you are moved by what you see beyond that which has controlled you. You can have cancer come your way or something that has controlled you, but you don't have to be moved at all. You've got insight. You are blinded to your cancer. You are blinded to the thing that is coming against you. You are blind to it. Because even though it is in your face, it will be outta your face.

But you've gotta get outta sight to get insight and you've gotta get insight to get foresight, which means that you gotta look beyond your present situation.

Moses, the Burning Bush, and the Voice

Moses saw a bush burning, an unusual phenomena. He saw a bush that refused to stop burning. But it was not the bush. It was not the fire. It was what was inside the fire that ultimately grabbed his attention.

So what did Moses do? Moses saw this great sight and he kept on walking. Then he looked at the fire that was coming from this bush, that is, he looked with his natural field of vision.

Then he said, "Now I will turn aside and see this great sight." In other words, "I have looked and I have beheld, now I will see this great sight." The word see there is to "look beyond my natural field of vision." And only when he moved out of sight into insight did God speak to him. You see, he walked by and nothing happened. Why didn't God say, "Hey, Moses," when he was looking? His field of vision did not give him access to anything else.

Your natural field of vision will not give you access to the voice of God. You are not going to hear God tapping on your shoulder. You might be in the middle of a revival, in the middle of a move of God, on a bus, or in your office…it doesn't matter. But while you are doing something, God will come to you.

It doesn't have to be a burning bush, but there will be something that you will be drawn to, something that will attract your attention. God could speak through a pole if He has to. He doesn't have to choose an incredible vessel. He can speak through whomever or whatever He likes. If you are going to become a prophetic voice you have got to move beyond trying to measure, trying to reason, trying to calculate, trying to work it out. You will never have access to the voice of God through your carnal and natural reasoning processes.

So Moses looks and turns aside to perceive. He looks beyond his field of vision at this great sight, and then God says, "Take your shoes off, for the ground you are standing on is holy ground now. It was not holy ground while you were observing, but it became holy when you drew near." In the place of holy ground and at the sound of God's voice, a desire was birthed within Moses—a desire to set God's people free. Before this encounter Moses had no desire to return to Egypt. He had lost his sight, and this is right where God wanted him. Because he lost his sight, now God could give him sight.

When God gives you a prophetic vision as to what you are going do or He calls you to do something, there is no personal desire attached to it. The voice of God will cancel out our desires and replace it with His desire. Most times this is a process. We don't normally give up our own desires so easily. When we finally come to the place where our eyes have seen things that we have never seen before and when our desires are converted into His desire, then we enter into a whole new realm of hope.

"For we are saved by hope: but hope that is seen is not hope: for what a man seeth, why doth he yet hope for? But if we hope for that we see not, then do we with patience wait for it" (Rom. 8:24-25 KJV). Real hope is based, not upon seeing what others see, but upon seeing what others do not see, and because we have seen the invisible we have the hope to wait for its coming.

Loss of Hope

You hear it over and over: People who are perfectly healthy the day they retire are pronounced dead within two years.

Why does it happen? Because their future is gone. They have nothing to live for any longer.

When people talk about faith, hope, and love (see 1 Cor. 13:13), they spend most of the time discussing faith and love. But they seem to forget what links them together—hope.

Prophets of God do not have a ministry of love, although they operate in love. They do not have a ministry of faith, although they operate by faith. Theirs is a ministry of hope—giving people something to live for.

One of the great Proverbs says, "Where there is no vision, the people perish" (Prov. 29:18 KJV). In other words, knowing God's plan is essential to your life. I am often asked, "Why would

God want to tell me something that will happen 20 or 30 years from now?" I believe God reveals His plan for us so that we may have confidence and security every day of our lives.

SUSTAINING POWER

Scripture is filled with dramatic accounts of people whose lives had actually been extended so God's promises to them could be fulfilled.

God had a plan for Paul's life. He said Paul was "a chosen vessel of Mine to bear My name before Gentiles, kings, and the children of Israel" (Acts 9:15).

During his missionary journeys, Paul was repeatedly threatened with death, yet God miraculously kept him alive. Once, when the Jews in Jerusalem were plotting to kill Paul, the voice of God came to him and said, "Be of good cheer, Paul; for as you have testified for Me in Jerusalem, so you must also bear witness at Rome" (Acts 23:11). In other words, your number isn't up yet!

The knowledge that he was going to witness in Rome sustained Paul in the face of great danger. Satan tried again and again to stop his journey. He was shipwrecked and placed in chains, but that did not discourage him. The voice of the Lord said there was something more he would accomplish.

Then it happened. Paul arrived in Rome and was placed under house arrest for two years—where he conveniently "received all who came to him, preaching the kingdom of God and teaching the things which concern the Lord Jesus Christ with all confidence, no one forbidding him" (Acts 28:30-31).

It makes no difference whether you are young or old. If you can catch the vision the Lord has for your life, He will keep you alive until you have completed the task.

Scripture tells us that "[King] David, after he had served the purpose of God in his own generation, died, [and] was laid beside his ancestors" (Acts 13:36 NRSV).

You may say, "But I'm not like David or Paul. I don't have a great calling on my life." Never underestimate the voice of the Lord. God took you out of the womb, breathed His life into you, and created a unique human being. He has raised you up for a purpose that no one else can accomplish.

A NEW DIMENSION

God will give you a glimpse of what lies far ahead if you are willing to enter a new spiritual dimension. That is what He did for the prophet Daniel. The Lord gave him a vision of things to come thousands of years into the future. God said:

> I have come to make you understand what will happen to your people in the latter days, for the vision refers to many days yet to come (Daniel 10:14).

King David prayed, "Show me Your ways, O Lord; teach me Your paths" (Ps. 25:4). In this generation God is restoring the prophetic ministry to the church for the purpose of sharing the ways of God. I believe He wants us to understand His thoughts and what He is preparing for the days and years ahead. When God's people understand what tomorrow holds, I believe they will move boldly forward in the power of the Spirit.

INEXPRESSIBLE

Once God speaks to you, it is only the beginning of His divine communication.

As you grow in grace, you are elevated to higher ground. The sounds become clear and distinct. His voice becomes the joy of your walk with Him.

At every act of obedience, God is communicating with you. He gives continual revelations to lead you from glory to glory as you achieve His plan for your life.

At times God may speak to you in words that are impossible to express. It may even take years to understand the meaning.

Or what He tells you may need to be held in confidence between you and God. The apostle Paul described how he was once "caught up into Paradise and heard inexpressible words, which it is not lawful for a man to utter" (2 Cor. 12:4).

Although the apostle received visions and revelations directly from God, he was not to boast about them. The Lord kept him humble by forcing him to deal with the problems of everyday life.

> *And lest I should be exalted above measure by the abundance of the revelations, a thorn in the flesh was given to me, a messenger of satan to buffet me, lest I be exalted above measure* (2 Corinthians 12:7).

God's plans and our emergencies often seem to be on different tracks, but the Lord knows exactly what we need. When the problems are the most severe, God proves Himself on behalf of individuals or nations.

Daniel was a man of faith and power, but he was thrown into a den of savage lions—a place of shame, dishonor, and danger. God's choice was to do something supernatural there. He closed the mouths of the lions, but he also addressed the root of the problem: the king's command to worship other gods. After Daniel survived the lions, the king made a decree that every person in the nation "must tremble and fear before the God of Daniel. For He is the living God, and steadfast forever; His kingdom is the one which shall not be destroyed, and His dominion shall endure to the end" (Dan. 6:26).

The same thing happened when Shadrach, Meshach, and Abednego were thrown into the furnace of fire. It seemed as if their time on earth had ended. But in the hour of their greatest need, the Son of Man made an appearance on their behalf.

> *King Nebuchadnezzar was astonished; and he rose in haste and spoke, saying to his counselors, "Did we not cast three men bound into the midst of the fire?" They answered and*

said to the king, "True, O king." "Look!" he answered, "I see four men loose, walking in the midst of the fire; and they are not hurt, and the form of the fourth is like the Son of God" (Daniel 3:24-25).

A HOLY HABITATION

One morning I told God in prayer, "Lord, it seems as if Your Church is being overwhelmed by the evils of satan and by such an ungodly society."

Then I heard the voice of God saying, "Look in the Scriptures. I have only just begun. When the enemy seems to be prevailing against the Kingdom, then I will make a judgment in favor of the saints."

The prophet Daniel said it long ago:

I was watching; and the same horn was making war against the saints, and prevailing against them, until the Ancient of Days came, and a judgment was made in favor of the saints of the Most High, and the time came for the saints to possess the kingdom (Daniel 7:21-22).

Even though satan seems to be coming against us, a time will come when the saints will prevail.

The Lord has shown me again and again that what is on the horizon is far greater than a breath of fresh air or a revival. And it is more than a visitation from above, in which the Lord comes, and then He leaves. We are going to experience a "habitation" of the Holy One. It will be permanent. He will come and reside!

The generation that God is raising up will cling to what the Lord provides. They will break down religious walls and say no to discord, contention, and strife.

Just when God is about to do something great, satan attempts to create havoc by attacking the children. I believe that the devil attempts to destroy a generation of children every time he realizes that God is about to unleash His awesome power. I believe he can sense it in the atmosphere.

When Christ was born, satan knew that a chosen generation was just ahead and that the blood of the cross would redeem man for eternity. So what did satan do? He planned an assault on innocent children.

When Herod heard that the wise men had followed the star that heralded the birth of a holy child, he was:

> *Exceedingly angry; and he sent forth and put to death all the male children who were in Bethlehem and in all its districts, from two years old and under, according to the time which he had determined from the wise men* (Matthew 2:16).

But God prevailed, and the generation that launched the Christian church emerged.

Nearly 2,000 years have passed, and satan is in the midst of his third onslaught. He is spewing out his wrath on millions of children while they are in their mothers' wombs. This is the murder of abortion.

The enemy knows that a generation is about to emerge that will usher in the King of kings. But God is speaking in these exciting times. For every child taken out by satan, I believe the Lord will raise up two to praise His name.

FOREVER STRONG

As we survey the battlefield, it may seem as if soldiers are falling, but the great conflict is just ahead. It is time for God's people to say, "Let God arise, let His enemies be scattered; let those also who hate Him flee before Him" (Ps. 68:1).

How can we fulfill the purpose of God in our generation? The story of Caleb holds the answer. Caleb was a man who knew and understood God, but he was surrounded by pessimists and unbelievers. When Moses sent spies to check out the promised land, Caleb's report was:

> *"Let us go up at once and take possession, for we are well able to overcome it." But the men who had gone up with him said,*

"We are not able to go up against the people, for they are stronger than we" (Numbers 13:30-31).

The people believed they were doomed to fail, so they refused to go into the promised land. You may say, "It's too bad that Caleb failed." But he didn't. Forty-five years later he was still serving God and was stronger than ever. At Gilgal, Caleb said to Joshua:

I was forty years old when Moses the servant of the Lord sent me from Kadesh Barnea to spy out the land, and I brought back word to him as it was in my heart (Joshua 14:7).

He explained how others brought back a different report. Then he said, "but I wholly followed the Lord my God" (Josh. 14:8). And listen to this! Caleb said:

Behold, the Lord has kept me alive, as He said, these forty-five years...and now, here I am this day, eighty-five years old. As yet I am as strong this day as on the day that Moses sent me; just as my strength was then, so now is my strength for war, both for going out and coming in (Joshua 14:10-11).

Caleb, even at that age, was ready to take on the giants. He said:

Now therefore, give me this mountain of which the Lord spoke in that day; for you heard in that day how the Anakim [giants] were there....It may be that the Lord will be with me, and I shall be able to drive them out as the Lord said (Joshua 14:12).

How did Caleb retain the strength of his youth? He never, ever turned his back on the voice of the Lord. As a result, God gave him a great inheritance (see Josh. 14:13).

You may feel that you are in a situation that makes it impossible to fulfill the promise of God. But don't give up. Keep His word alive, and the Lord will preserve you and allow you to see a stunning victory.

When Will It Happen?

I shudder to think what would have become of my life if I had never heard the voice of God. His messenger came to me when I was bleeding and dying in a filthy gutter outside that club in Port Elizabeth.

But with my salvation He gave me a promise that has sustained me. No matter where I travel, I can still hear the words God spoke when Pastor Pretorius lifted me out of the waters of baptism. The Lord not only called me to the ministry, but He said, "None of your household will go to the grave without salvation."

When my parents resisted me because of the radical turnaround I experienced, I wondered, *How can it happen? How can they ever be free?* The tension in our home felt like a wire that had been stretched to the breaking point.

But God began to give me signs of encouragement. A few months after my conversion, my sister, Shelley, saw that the transformation in my life was genuine. She asked questions about Jesus and finally gave her heart to God. She began attending church with me.

Day after day I prayed that a miracle would happen in the lives of my parents. But there was no response. All I could cling to was the promise I heard God speak.

While I served my "apostolic apprenticeship" as a new convert, and when I was on duty in the South African army, I was increasingly concerned for my mother. She had become crippled with arthritis. It broke my heart to see her in pain, with stiffness, swelling, and inflammation of the joints.

One day when I was on the staff of the Pentecostal Protestant Church in Port Elizabeth, I said to my mother, "Why don't you come to church with me tonight?" An older evangelist, Reverend Arthur Nipper, was conducting special services.

I was surprised when both my mother *and* my father came with me. The power of God was so strong during that meeting that I was expecting a miracle to take place in their lives. But they left the building with no response.

Later that night I was thrilled when Mom took me aside and said, "Kim, do you think you could have that minister come and pray for me?"

"Of course," I assured her.

The next day evangelist Nipper drove to our home and anointed my mother with oil and prayed for her healing.

"Something is happening," she said. The swelling in her body began to subside. "The pain is gone!" she exclaimed.

Instantly, my mother was healed. Several days later, while she was thanking God for her miracle, she prayed the sinner's prayer and asked that the blood of Christ would cleanse her from her sin. In the middle of the night, while she was reading the Book of Acts, she received the baptism of the Holy Spirit.

My father was another story. He was still a skeptic. It seemed that nothing we could say or do would bring him into the Kingdom. "But, God, You promised!" I kept praying even after I moved to Durban, was married, and began traveling in ministry.

Then came that devastating moment in 1986 at the air terminal in Canada. My family was with me, and we were about to pick up tickets to fly to a meeting in the United States. I'll never forget the concerned look on the woman's face at the counter when she asked, "Are you Mr. Clement?"

"Yes, I am," I replied. "Is there some kind of problem?"

"I have been asked to give you this message. Your father has died in South Africa."

Instantly, I became nauseated, and tears rushed to my eyes. But in that moment the Lord said again, "Do you remember My word?" Of course I did. Years before, God had promised, "None of your household will go to the grave without salvation."

The clerk looked puzzled when I told her, "It's impossible! God told me he is not going to die until he believes as I do."

"Well, I don't know anything about that," she said, "but this is the message I was told to give you. I'm very sorry."

It is difficult to explain, but when God reminded me of His voice, He also gave me a peace and serenity that was beyond description.

When I reached my mother by phone in Uitenhage, she was obviously upset.

"Tell me what has happened to Daddy," I said. "I was told that he died."

"No," she said. "We told them to tell you that he is dying. The doctors have given him only a few hours to live." I learned that my father had suffered a massive stroke and was in a coma, totally paralyzed. "They are telling me that he will never walk or talk again," she said.

At that moment, God gave me a special word, which I tried to tell her, but she kept interrupting. "Kim, they told me he's not going to make it. It is the most severe type of stroke anyone can have."

Through her tears I said, "Mom, listen to me! Don't talk like that. He is going to make it because I had a word from God."

She calmed down long enough for me to tell her, "God said that he's going to live and not die. He's going to walk and talk."

I repeated what God said. I was so sure of what I had heard God saying to me that I did not cancel my speaking schedule. Instead, I continued my ministry and kept in touch with my mother by phone.

After several days in a coma, my father suddenly opened his eyes. He began to speak. He began to move his arms and legs. My mother called and said, "Kim, your father asked me to pray with him. He asked Jesus to come into his heart!" That was one of the happiest moments of my life. God's words to me had been fulfilled.

Later I flew back to South Africa to visit him. It was difficult to see him in a wheelchair, but God was doing a great work of healing. He called me to his room and said, "Kim, I want everything God has for me. I would like to be filled with the Spirit. Will you pray with me?"

Not only did he receive a great spiritual experience, but the Spirit of God swept over both of us. For years my father and I had had nothing in common at all. Now there was an incredible connection bonding us together.

Not only did he become a believer, but he was filled with the Spirit and God has extended his life. For years my father lived a fairly normal life; he spoke and could walk until his death in 1996.

Death Was Defied

I will never fully understand the mysteries of how God works. My older brother, Barry, was diagnosed with Hodgkin's disease, a type of cancer that affects the lymph nodes. Like my father, he was given only a short time to live. He refused God until the very end.

As his condition was deteriorating, the Lord allowed me to be at his side. Again, I prayed, "Lord, You told me they would all be free!"

I was able to pray with Barry as he called on Jesus. Two months later I had the joy of baptizing him in water. He was also healed totally of his cancer. To me, there is no question that death was defied because of the voice of God.

My younger brother, David, was the last in our family to be touched by the power of God. He came to God in 1992.

I wish I could tell you that when you hear the voice of God, everything will suddenly be perfect. Members of my family continue to struggle with the issues of life because sin still stalks the earth. There is one thing, however, on which we can depend. God said, "My word...shall not return to Me void, but it shall

accomplish what I please, and it shall prosper in the thing for which I sent it" (Isa. 55:11).

It is my prayer that you will *hear* the voice of God.
I pray that you will *believe* the word of God.
Start today to *act* upon it in faith.
I pray that you will *discover* the secrets of the prophetic.
It is your destiny to *become* the voice of God to those who are crying out for His life.